D0408893

CALGARY PUBLIC LIBRARY

• JUN ⁃ 2009

SPECIAL MESSAGE TO READERS

This book is published under the auspices of

THE ULVERSCROFT FOUNDATION

(registered charity No. 264873 UK)

Established in 1972 to provide funds for research, diagnosis and treatment of eye diseases. Examples of contributions made are: —

A Children's Assessment Unit at
Moorfield's Hospital, London.

•

Twin operating theatres at the
Western Ophthalmic Hospital, London.

•

A Chair of Ophthalmology at the
Royal Australian College of Ophthalmologists.

•

The Ulverscroft Children's Eye Unit at the
Great Ormond Street Hospital For Sick Children,
London.

You can help further the work of the Foundation by making a donation or leaving a legacy. Every contribution, no matter how small, is received with gratitude. Please write for details to:

**THE ULVERSCROFT FOUNDATION,
The Green, Bradgate Road, Anstey,
Leicester LE7 7FU, England.
Telephone: (0116) 236 4325**

**In Australia write to:
THE ULVERSCROFT FOUNDATION,
c/o The Royal Australian and New Zealand
College of Ophthalmologists,
94-98 Chalmers Street, Surry Hills,
N.S.W. 2010, Australia**

Anne Nolan was born in Dublin in 1950, the second eldest of eight children. The family moved from Dublin to Blackpool in 1961 shortly after which they started to tour as the Singing Nolans. Later the Nolan Sisters went on to achieve massive chart success with hits like *I'm in the Mood for Dancing* which became a success all over the world.

Anne has two daughters and lives in Blackpool.

ANNE'S SONG

Anne Nolan, the eldest of the Nolan Sisters, seemed to have a glamorous, exciting life — a dream come true for any young singer. The six singing sisters went from the Blackpool club circuit to achieve massive success, and supported a stellar string of stars from Cliff Richard to Frank Sinatra. The Nolans travelled the world to play for their adoring fans. But behind the spotlights lay a dark reality: her tyrannical father was hell-bent on destroying Anne's innocence. His actions cast a shadow over Anne's life, stunting her relationships, contributing to the breakdown of her marriage and almost costing her the unconditional love of her two adored daughters. Unflinchingly honest, *Anne's Song* is the brutal truth behind the carefully cultivated image that was the Nolans.

ANNE NOLAN
WITH RICHARD BARBER

♦

ANNE'S SONG

Complete and Unabridged

ULVERSCROFT
Leicester

First published in Great Britain in 2008 by
Century
The Random House Group Limited, London

First Large Print Edition
published 2009
by arrangement with
The Random House Group Limited, London

The moral right of the author has been asserted

This book is a work of non-fiction based on the life, experiences and recollections of Anne Nolan. In some cases names of people have been changed to protect the privacy of others. The author has stated to the publishers that, except in such respects, the contents of this book are true.

Copyright © 2008 by Anne Nolan
All rights reserved

British Library CIP Data

Nolan, Anne.
    Anne's song
    1. Nolan, Anne. 2. Nolans (Musical group).
    3. Women singers- -Great Britain- -Biography.
    4. Singers- -Great Britain- -Biography.
    5. Large type books.
    I. Title II. Barber, Richard, *1947 Nov. 26 –*
    782.4′2164′092–dc22

    ISBN 978–1–84782–632–9

Published by
F. A. Thorpe (Publishing)
Anstey, Leicestershire

Set by Words & Graphics Ltd.
Anstey, Leicestershire
Printed and bound in Great Britain by
T. J. International Ltd., Padstow, Cornwall

This book is printed on acid-free paper

To John Kent for his initial help and encouragement in writing this book.

To my Auntie Teresa for her love, for always being there when I needed her and for giving myself, my daughters and the dog a home when we didn't have one.

To my mum for her unconditional love and sacrifice throughout all her life.

I dedicate this book to my two wonderful daughters Amy and Alex for their understanding, for their love, for giving me a reason to go on when I was at my lowest and for giving meaning to my life

Contents

Prologue

We'd just finished a performance at the Brunswick Working Men's Club in Blackpool. It was 1967. We were known as the Singing Nolans then. There were my mother and father, my elder brother Tommy, me, Denise and Maureen, my younger brother Brian, Linda and Bernie, and Coleen — although she wasn't yet three at that point.

The three youngest girls went on first, did their act and were then taken home by my Aunt Teresa in a taxi. Then the rest of us performed our act: although we'd all join in on most songs, each of us also had a solo. Mine was 'It Had To Be You', Maureen's was Nancy Sinatra's 'These Boots Were Made For Walking'. We got a great reception. We always did. People would whistle and clap and cheer. The audience loved us. We always got a standing ovation.

Normally, at the end of the evening, I'd share a taxi or a lift of some sort with my brothers and sisters. But, on this occasion, my father drew me to one side and asked if I'd wait behind and go back home with him in his car. There was something, he said, he wanted to discuss with me. I did as he asked but I wondered what on earth he wanted to say that couldn't be said in front of anyone else.

It was only about five minutes from the club to where we lived, but suddenly he took a wrong turning and then another. We seemed to be going on some sort of a detour.

I said, 'What are you doing?'

Dad looked sideways at me. 'I just want to have a word with you,' he said. 'In private.'

I wasn't scared but I wondered what was going on. He slowed down, parked the car in a side street and turned off the engine. Now he was facing me. He didn't bother with any preliminaries.

'I was thinking,' he said, almost matter-of-factly, 'why don't the two of us run away together?'

I laughed, half embarrassed, half not understanding what he was on about.

He said, 'Because you know I love you, don't you?'

This was beginning to scare me. I said, 'Yes,' trying to keep my voice sounding as calm as possible. 'You're my dad.'

'Oh no,' he said, 'not like that.'

I was getting panicky. I said, 'Why are you saying this? What about Mum? Don't you love Mum?'

2

'Yes, I do love your mum,' he said, 'but in a different way.' I was staring straight ahead at the street in front of me. I wouldn't look at him, I didn't want to, but out of the corner of my eye I could see he was still gripping the steering wheel with both hands.

I didn't speak. It was as though my mind couldn't take all of this in. Was my own father really suggesting that we should suddenly disappear and set up home together as a couple, effectively as man and wife? It was beyond my comprehension.

I thought my head would explode and then the most curious thing happened. I seemed to be vacating my own body, as if I were somewhere else, as if I were no longer in the car with him. I suppose I was, quite literally, going through an out-of-body experience. I'm not sure, but I may even have fainted for a few seconds. I can only describe it as a feeling of no longer being there.

I couldn't hear my father any more, although I was somehow aware he was still talking. I couldn't make any sense of his words. My mind must have been insulating me from their full implication. I just couldn't bear to take on board what he was suggesting.

It was then I began thinking that either he was mad or perhaps just terribly ill. I started to feel physically unwell. I thought I was going to be sick. Was my own father serious about the suggestion that he and I could have a life together as partners? It was the most horrendous thing I'd ever heard. I think I started to cry.

In time, he must have realised that I was traumatised, that I was in a state of complete and utter shock, because he switched the engine back on and, without further ado, we drove home in silence. He never referred to this incident again.

Dad was forty. I was sixteen.

★　★　★

Of all my brothers and sisters, Brian is the one who most minds about my writing this book. He feels — and I respect this — that the image of the Nolans should be left intact. However, I feel even more strongly that I want to tell *my* story. I've lived with the shame and the guilt of what happened to me for long enough. I'm not a vengeful person, and I'm genuinely sorry if a few illusions are shattered in the process, but I've kept my secret to myself for too long. Now it's Anne's turn.

1

An Irish Childhood

Everyone knew my father by his first name, and everyone knew Tommy Nolan. Whether in Dublin or Blackpool, he was hugely popular, both as a performer and as a man. He was easy to talk to and naturally charming, but it was more than that. He had the kind of personality that made people gravitate towards him. There was something magnetic about him. Men liked him because he was one of the lads and women were clearly attracted to him. I didn't understand the implications of that when I was little but, in my mind's eye, there were always women around him.

Despite the big public persona, though, he chose to keep his private life private — but then, he had plenty to be private about.

My mother was christened Mary but was always known as Maureen. (My sister, Maureen, was christened Marie. I have an elder brother, Tommy, named after my dad and that's as much a tradition in Ireland as girls called Mary often being known by another name!) Mum was eighty-one when she died just after Christmas 2007. She'd been in the grip of Alzheimer's, lying in bed in a home and unable to follow anything that was going on or to recognise even members of her own family. Now and then, she'd seem to have a lucid moment when she'd say a word that made you think she might know who you were, but the moment soon passed

She was a real beauty when she was young, very slim with dark hair and dark eyes, only a little over five feet tall. She had the most beguiling voice, and at seventeen she won a scholarship to a music college in Dublin. She could have trained as an opera singer, but she wanted to do musical comedy — and have babies. As it was, she never took up her place.

She met my father when he was singing at a corporate event in Dublin. One of the female singers was ill, so, at the last moment, my mother was booked to take her place. Although she was only twenty, her regular job was at the Capitol cinema where she'd come on stage between movies and sing to the audience. My father was the same age as my mother and obviously the attraction was mutual. A year later, they were man and wife.

She was a warm, caring woman, although not the sort who'd kiss and cuddle her children for no reason. While she was naturally gentle and soft, if we pushed her — and we did — she could be fiery, but it was always soon forgotten. Her bark was worse than her bite and she'd hardly ever smack us; and yet, it would have been understandable if she were short-tempered. She must have been exhausted most of the time. She had eight children in the end, five of us under the age of six at one stage. No one could have been kinder if you were ill. In fact, I sometimes used to wish I was just ill enough because then Mum would make a fuss of me. She'd wrap you in a blanket on the couch and bring you hot drinks. I loved that.

Like my mother, my father had dark colouring, but he had an angular face. It's difficult for a child to judge, but I'd say he was a good-looking man. He was strict, someone who liked things done his way, and he had about him an extraordinary presence. My mum would rant and rave and scream at us if we were playing her up — and we just ignored her. My dad didn't have to say a word. Just one look from him and you stopped what you were doing. You might imagine that we were frightened that he'd lash out at us if we didn't do as we'd been asked, but it wasn't like that at all. He never hit us. He didn't need to. The man possessed innate power.

What hung in the air was the unknown possibility of what he might do if one of us stepped seriously out of line. Some people have the ability to let you know that, without having to raise a finger in anger, they can only be pushed so far and woe betide. My father was one of them. So, while part of me was pleased to have a strong provider and protector looking out for his family, there lurked in the depths of his personality something unseen. And, had I been able to articulate it back then, it scared me.

If you had a headache, my mum was the one who'd come and put her hand on your forehead. She was kind and lovely, always there for us. We all adored her — in fact, we took her for granted, I now see — but if something was wrong, if there was some sort of a crisis in your life, my dad was the one you'd go to. He was indisputably the head of the household, the person who would sort out any trouble on your behalf. He was strong, protective, a man of the world, a natural leader.

Wherever he went, everybody loved him. If he had any enemies, I was never aware of them. Even now, I might be speaking to someone who knew him and they'll tell me how much they admired him. He was the life and soul of any gathering but never loud, never a show-off. If people asked him to sing when he was out somewhere, he'd always oblige in his deep, rich voice. He was always the pivotal person in any group, the man to whom people listened when he spoke. He had natural authority.

I was never worried he'd say something foolish when we were out with him. He'd never embarrass you because he always somehow knew the right thing to say. He was also generous. If he went out anywhere, he'd always be the first to stand a round of drinks. At home, he was quieter. You'd often find him, alone in a room, listening to the radio or his record collection or reading. There was an introspective side to him that you'd never have known if you met him in a public place.

There were plenty of good times. At meals, for example, he'd often tell us stories from his childhood or about his time in show business when he first started out. One of my favourites was about when he was twelve and was out with his two best mates. They were cycling in Dublin and headed off down to the Liffey where my father failed to brake in time and plunged straight into the river. He couldn't swim and had to be rescued by a passer-by, otherwise he might well have drowned. That always seemed very dramatic to me and he told the story so well.

He was also a naturally witty man, like his mother before him, with a wonderful sense of humour and an original way of looking at the world. He'd have us all laughing. He was well educated. He'd been taught by the Christian Brothers who were extremely strict and who expected complete concentration from their students. They instilled in him a great love of history, and particularly the history of Ireland which he passed on to us. He was fiercely patriotic and not a great fan of the English, of course. He gave us our love of reading — in particular Charles Dickens — and music.

He adored his family almost, I would now say, to the point of being obsessed by us. My mother was a huge part of my father's life, but I always got the impression he was more bothered about his children than he was about his wife. Certainly, he never showed her any affection in public, although that was partly explained by the fact that most adults weren't openly demonstrative to each other in public in those days. I think he loved her in his way, but I never even saw them hold hands. I don't ever remember them arguing when we were young.

He was more obviously affectionate towards us, his children. He certainly didn't like it if he felt anyone was rivalling him for that affection. We were extremely close to our Aunt

Teresa, my mother's youngest sister who was only sixteen when I was born. I think he was a bit jealous of how fond we were of her. She was almost like a big sister to me, but then, because she's never had children of her own, I think she regards all of us as her surrogate children. She's always been kind and protective and loving as well as extremely pretty, with the same colouring as my mother's. I regard her as my rock and have done all my life.

My father was a smart man, always neatly dressed. His trousers were never without a crease and worn either with a short-sleeved shirt in summer or a meticulously ironed long-sleeved one in winter. He shaved every day without fail. His hair was worn short and brushed. He had lovely nails that he kept spotlessly clean and clipped. He'd polish his shoes until they shone and taught us to polish ours, too. He spoke well, and he cut a figure even though he can't have been more than five foot eight and very thin at that. He never put on weight throughout his whole adult life, although he loved his food and drink.

As I was to discover, however, there was another side to the man, a dark, disturbed side.

Looking back now, I realise I didn't really get to know my father properly for the first ten years of my life. He worked all day as a bookkeeper for a glass company in Dublin and then he'd be off at night, singing in a local club called the Royclla or travelling with The Morris Mulcahy Band, a jazz group well known in Ireland at the time.

There was no one my father liked better than Frank Sinatra. He played his records all the time so that there wasn't a Sinatra song we didn't know inside out. In fact, on the radio he'd be introduced as Ireland's Frank Sinatra and that's also how he'd be billed on posters. He was a crooner with a great range and a natural baritone voice. Sometimes, he'd be called Tommy 'Cool Water' Nolan after a song called 'Cool Clear Water' that was popular at the time. When television came to Ireland, my dad and The Bachelors, Ireland's top male vocal group, were on the very first show broadcast by Telefis Eireann, the national TV station.

My mother was a soprano with a beautiful, clear tone. She favoured songs from shows like *Oklahoma!* or *Carousel*, but she'd also sing arias like 'One Fine Day' from *Madame Butterfly*. Later on, when the family moved to England, she and Dad would sometimes sing together in the working men's clubs and hotels in the north-west. They were billed as Tommy and Maureen, the Sweethearts of

Song. They might sing 'My Heart and I', for instance, and people would go mad for them.

Mum was slim when she married my father but, after eight pregnancies, her figure began to fill out. She always dressed up if we went anywhere for the evening or if she was on a singing engagement, but at home, she'd just wear a frock. She had too much to do to bother with appearances if she was indoors. When we were young, she wouldn't have dreamt of going out without wearing make-up, but, as she got older, she seemed to mind less. However, we weren't having any of that. We'd always persuade her to put it on. She had lovely skin — she still has now — and I think she thought she could get away without make-up, but she always looked better if she'd made the effort. The same was true of her hair. By the time I was in my twenties, she'd let me do her hair and make-up for her.

Even allowing for the way he later treated her, my mother loved my father until the day he died. He was certainly fond of her, but whether he was in love with her we'll never know. He wasn't a man who was free with his emotions. She was pregnant with my brother Tommy when they married. Marriage would have been insisted upon; it would have been judged shameful in Ireland at the end of the forties to have a child out of wedlock. They were both only twenty-one.

★ ★ ★

I was born at Hollies Street Maternity Hospital in Dublin on 12 November 1950, and christened Anne Barbara Maria. I was the second child; Tommy had been born in July of the previous year. Eventually, there would be eight of us: six girls and two boys. My mother and I spent my very early childhood living with my maternal grandparents, Miles and Kathleen Breslin. My parents couldn't afford a house of their own at that stage and hadn't yet been allocated council accommodation. I'm sure they longed for us all to be together under one roof, although I never remember them saying this to us. Adults wouldn't discuss something like that in front of children back then.

I loved living with my grandparents. My grandmother called me her Madonna. I was the first granddaughter in the family and she made a tremendous fuss of me, as did my Aunt Teresa. I was spoilt to death. I saw my dad and brother every now and then, but I can't say I missed them. My mum would sometimes go and stay with my father at his parents' house on the other side of the city. I don't suppose they found it ideal, but I was perfectly happy.

Nana Breslin indulged me from dawn to dusk. I remember being fond of beetroot, for example, which she used to buy fresh from the market. She might be preparing it for a meal and I'd sit beside her and eat as much of it as I could, but she never told me off. My mum might come into the kitchen and say, 'Don't do that. It's Nana's,' but my grandmother would reply, 'Oh, leave her. She's fine.'

Tommy and my dad lived with his mother, Mary Nolan, in a flat above a corner shop in Clontarf, quite a smart seaside resort to the north of Dublin. She was lovely and would always make me laugh. She'd wander round the house humming with a cigarette hanging out of her mouth. However, I think she'd been spoilt when she was young. Certainly, she wasn't happy if she didn't get her own way. She was given to throwing tantrums; she'd flounce out of the room and go and sit on her own in her bedroom.

Her husband Thomas, by all accounts a kind, caring man, had died when my dad was twelve, leaving Tommy as the only male in the household — he had two older sisters, Shelagh and Doreen. I think his mother put a lot of pressure on him too young to transform himself into the man of the house, and I've often wondered whether what was effectively the loss of his childhood shaped the character of the person he later became.

Gran Nolan and my mother never really got on. I don't think she thought Mum was good enough for her son, but then I don't think any girl would have been. Even so, she'd taunt my mother by talking about my dad's previous girlfriends. There was a particular one called Maud Quinn who was quite posh and belonged to the local tennis club. I think Gran Nolan would have preferred her as a daughter-in-law. Not that my mother took any notice of all this: it was water off a duck's back.

I was four when my parents were given a terraced council house on the Ballygael Road in an area of Dublin called Finglas. Denise and Maureen had been born by then. Denise is two years younger than me and Maureen three and a half years younger. I'm as close to Denise as I am to Tommy, probably because they were born either side of me.

Tommy's always been very extrovert, very funny, but if he has something on his mind that's worrying him, he'll either ignore it or blurt it out, pretending it's a joke when we all know it isn't. He's been like that for as long as I can remember. We fought like cat and dog when we were young, but we've always been very close. One Christmas, I remember, our parents bought each of us boxing gloves and we'd spar with one another. I usually won, not because I was stronger but because I hit Tommy with all my might while he held back because I was a girl. He's always been protective of me.

Tommy was a very good-looking boy with dark hair and eyes to match and he grew into a handsome young man. As a child, Denise was very cute with dark curly hair and brown eyes; as an adult she's the one who looks most like our mother. She's very placid, very loving. She's the kindest person I know, someone who would never, ever forget a birthday or an anniversary. If it's someone's birthday, she'll be the one who arranges the party, who gets everyone together, who buys the cake. Every spare minute she has, she goes to visit our mum and she's not shy of keeping us up to the task, either. She can be fiery, and too sensitive sometimes for her own good which means she's always been easily hurt, but she doesn't hold grudges. Family means everything to Denise.

My only abiding memory of living in Finglas is of the babysitter my parents would employ when they were out in the evenings on singing engagements. On one occasion, this girl — she can barely have been a teenager — got bored with sitting in our house and wanted to take me over the road to where she lived. The only problem was what to do with Denise who was just a toddler and who couldn't tag along like me. So she tied Denise to the bedpost by her hair. I may have been young but I wasn't standing by and letting that happen to my sister. I marched straight upstairs and released her. People who meet me might describe me as quiet, but that doesn't mean I'm timid. I'm a strong character and I know the difference between right and wrong. With one exception, I've never let anyone control me.

Not long before we moved out of the house in Finglas in June 1954, my sister Maureen was born. Maureen's the one on whom everyone can offload their troubles. She doesn't get riled; she's the family peace-keeper, a person who never likes to think badly of anyone; she's been like that since childhood. She's also the family beauty, no question. She had hazel eyes and mid-brown hair with a slim figure. And she was always smiling. Anyone who met her was always attracted to both her looks and to her personality.

★ ★ ★

We moved to the St Anne's Estate in Raheny when I was five. Finglas had a reputation for being pretty rough, but Raheny, while still a council estate, was a cut above; we were moving up in the world. By then, there were six of us: my parents, Tommy, me, Denise and Maureen. Hence the move; we were a rapidly expanding family.

Ours was the corner house next to some sort of electricity substation fenced off behind a large locked gate. I was a bit of a tomboy and I'd think nothing of climbing over this gate, although it was forbidden and potentially very dangerous. There was also a big derelict mansion not far away, in a place we called Seven Hills. I'd be down there with my little group of friends, climbing in and out of its broken windows — or we'd go off to a new estate that was being built and get inside when the workmen had gone. We'd also shin up trees and then spit on people as they passed underneath.

I was at the local girls' Catholic junior school where I made lots of friends and enjoyed my book work, but the highlight for me was always the school concert where we'd perform for the teachers and our parents. I can still recall the material of the dress I wore when I had to tap dance with a group of other six-year-olds. It was made of bright red net and covered in sequins with a skirt that stuck out. I felt like a film star, someone out of a Fred Astaire and Ginger Rogers movie. It's one of the best memories of my childhood.

When I think back to my early years growing up in Ireland, I was rarely indoors. I'd either be at school or playing outside with my friends, often still eating the last of my tea as I ran out the door. I was meant to be in the street outside our house where I'd play hopscotch or skipping games, but, being a little wild thing, I'd be off and getting up to all sorts in the fields that surrounded our estate. We were never supervised, but life seemed somehow so much safer back then.

I'd only come home again when it was time to go to bed: at seven in the winter, which I hated because it seemed so early, but eight in the summer because of the light evenings. In bad weather, we'd stay indoors and, if my dad was around, he'd read to us or we'd look at comics or draw or listen to the radio. There was always music and singing in the house. Each of us kids must have inherited Mum and Dad's musical ability because a song only had to come on the radio and we'd all start singing along, unconsciously able to pick up the right harmonies. In time, we were given little bits of homework by the teachers at school. It was a wonderful carefree kind of a childhood. Our parents were there if we needed them, but we were allowed to be what we wanted to be. We might not have been rich in terms of material possessions, but we were loved and we were happy. There's no price you can put on that.

Sometimes Dad would take us in his old banger out to Howth Head or we'd go by steam train to the seaside at Bray, where we'd sit on the grass on the promenade and eat fish and chips; or we'd walk into Dollymount and buy sweets, and then stay on the beach all day and eat the picnic Mum had made: bread and jam washed down with bottles of water or lemonade for a special treat. We couldn't swim, but we'd play in the sea and we never came to any harm. It was an uncomplicated, contented early childhood with no foretaste of the dark days to come.

When Tommy and I went to school down the road, we'd run home at lunchtime to listen to a radio programme, a daily soap opera, called *The Kennedys of Castle Ross* while Mum made the food. She was a plain cook. It might be sausages, beans and potatoes or, one of her favourites, a joint of gammon served with mashed potato and cabbage or curly kale. We loved her banana sandwiches, and I remember Denise was particularly partial to her rice pudding. At the weekend, she'd always make a huge pan of stew. I don't recall her teaching us how to cook, although, when we were older, we were taught how to bake. I remember my Dublin days as an idyllic upbringing for a child, even if money was tight — and that was something that children don't really understand, or need to, when they're growing up.

When I must have been no more than six, Nana Breslin died. It was a terrible shock. She had an asthma attack on a bus that brought on a heart attack. She was only fifty-two. I remember someone coming to our house when I was in bed. I heard voices at the front door and suddenly my mother let out a piercing scream. I could hear her sobbing her heart out, but nobody came to tell us what was going on or why she was so upset. So I got out of bed and called through the banisters, asking what the matter was. My dad said, 'Oh, it's just your mammy. She's fine now.'

The next day, I asked him again. He said, 'Your nana's gone to heaven.' And that was that. I didn't really understand what I'd been told, but every time I tried to talk about it, someone changed the subject. I wasn't allowed to go to the funeral, so I never got the chance to say goodbye to her. Eventually, my granddad, Miles, got married again to a lovely woman called Madge.

I think it took my mother a long time to get over the loss of Nana Breslin, but that is only a presumption I've arrived at with hindsight. She never, ever discussed her feelings with us. Instead, she was kept constantly busy round the house. If she was in a good mood, she'd let us join in and help her. She might suddenly shout out, 'Right. Who's for polishing the floor then?' You'd expect most children to make a dash for the door, but not in our house. The chorus of 'Me! Me! Me!' must have been heard halfway down the street as we rushed to volunteer. Mum would tie rags to our feet and we'd skate and slide the full length of the hall floor, polishing it in the process. If we'd been good, she'd give us money for sweets.

There were two rooms on the ground floor on the right as you came in the front door. The one that overlooked the street was kept for best occasions; the other was a family room. There was a kitchen opposite. Upstairs, there was a bathroom with a toilet and three bedrooms. I shared with Denise and Maureen. Tommy and later Brian had the second room, and our parents had the other. It was a long time before any of us had a bed to ourselves and certainly never when we lived in Ireland.

We girls used to play a game in our bedroom called Standing On Knees. Denise and I would sit on the bed and raise our knees. Maureen — and Linda later on — would take our hands and climb on, then we'd let go and they'd have to stand balanced on our knees without falling off. Or one of us would sit at one end of the bed with another at the other end and we'd join hands and rock backwards and forwards, like a swing-boat. Of course there would sometimes be arguments, many of them started by me. I was a tearaway, happy to pick fights with anyone. I daresay there was a bit of hair-pulling, too — it would be surprising if that hadn't happened, as we were all living on top of each other — but we were very close, each other's best friends, which is how it remained throughout our career.

Our next-door neighbours in Raheny were the McMahon family. There were seven children, the oldest a girl called Mary who was two years older than me. She taught me to ride a bike and I took my First Communion with her brother Padraic when we were both seven. It was a great and special day in my life with visiting relatives and friends showering gifts and money on us in the old Irish tradition. That night, Dad took me to the Royella, the nightclub where he was the resident singer. He sat me at the side of the stage where everybody made a great fuss of me; he bought me a bottle of pop and I was allowed to stay and watch his act. I felt very grown-up.

It was also around this time that we got a black-and-white television, the first people on the estate to own a set. I was so transfixed by it that I was happy just watching the test card on the screen when I got home from school and before programmes started in the early evening. My favourites were *The Flowerpot Men* and *The Woodentops*; later on, it would be *Emergency Ward 10* and *Dr Kildare*; I was deeply in love with Richard Chamberlain.

My second brother, Brian, arrived after we'd moved to Raheny. He turned out to be as quiet as Tommy was noisy. He was shy and introverted to the point of being scared of his own shadow. He had a big fort and would spend hours playing with his soldiers on his own. In 1958, Linda arrived; that makes her eight years younger than me. I never remember my mother being pregnant and it was never discussed. It was just that every eighteen months or so, there was a new baby in the house. Linda was the polar opposite of

Brian: an outgoing, sunny child we nick-named Dublin Molly because of her deep voice and strong accent.

This was also the year that Denise made *her* First Communion. I behaved appallingly because this was her day. I'd been pampered when it had been my turn the previous year, but still I was jealous of all the attention she was getting. In a deliberate act of spite, I broke one of her dolls by throwing it on the ground and smashing one of its arms. When she found out, my mother smacked me on my bare legs, something I thoroughly deserved. I went stamping up to our bedroom and then screamed insults at Denise and my parents out of the window as they took her off to the Royella as part of her special day. However, just as Tommy was protective of me, so I usually felt the same about Denise.

There was a hut in a field near us for the local football team. Inside, it was divided down the middle so the two opposing teams could get changed into and out of their kit. When I was seven, a group of girls and another of boys dreamed up the idea of going to this changing room, taking off all our clothes and then one boy and one girl would step outside and show each other their bits and pieces. We knew it was naughty, but without really understanding why. Because

Denise was my little sister, I wouldn't let her come on this so-called adventure. So she went to our mum to tell her that something bad was happening. The next thing I knew, my mother was dragging me home, a small hearth brush in her hand with which she was trying to whack me across the bottom as I dodged out of her range. As it happens, it hadn't reached my turn in the game to reveal all to one of the local boys. I dread to think what she'd have done if she'd witnessed that. She gave me a good smacking when we got home and I was sent to bed with no tea. I sobbed myself to sleep. After a little while, though — and this was typical of my mum — she came and woke me up with something to eat and gave me a big cuddle. I'd done something wrong. I'd been punished. It was all over.

2

Abandoned

I was seven when I first started getting pains in my legs. They weren't sharp, stabbing pains, more like dull aches, the kind of pains you'd get if you'd been cycling all day. They were never so bad that I'd be unable to walk but I would have to take painkillers to help me get to sleep. Nobody seemed to know what was causing them. Was it rheumatism? Growing pains? Polio? The doctors couldn't make up their minds. I was taken to the local hospital on a weekly basis where I'd be given a painkilling injection, but the pains persisted. In time, they did discover I had some sort of heart murmur, so then they thought I might be suffering from rheumatic fever, but I was never given any medication and nor did I feel ill.

The pains weren't bad enough to keep me off school and life carried on as before. In the summer of 1960, when she was pregnant with Bernie, Mum went on a trip to England where she stayed with her uncle, Joe Hayes. On her return to Dublin, she was full of her trip, and I remember her talking to my dad about it.'

'It was lovely,' she told him. 'I met some really nice people. And there are so many clubs, Tommy. We could make a real good living there.'

Apparently, Uncle Joe had taken Mum to the British Legion Club one evening where she'd volunteered to sing a song. A man called Fred Daly, a friend of Joe's, was in the club that night. So impressed was he with my mother's singing, he tried to persuade her that her future lay on that side of the water.

Dad wasn't convinced. 'Where would we live?' he asked. 'Our home and friends are in Dublin. You can't just uproot a family like ours and dump them in the middle of a strange town in a strange country.'

Mum persisted. 'Fred said he'd put us up in his house until we found our own place.'

Dad laughed. 'And did you warn him we're like the tribe of Israel?'

'Be serious, Tommy,' she said. 'I mean it. You and me singing together? We'd clean up in the working men's clubs.'

'But what about my radio work?' said Dad. He had a regular weekday morning show on Radio Eireann on which he'd play records by Frank Sinatra, Dean Martin and so on as well as singing himself with a live band. 'It's a good income and popular enough to last a long time yet.'

For the moment, at least, his argument won the day and Mum appeared to drop the idea.

In October 1960, Bernie was born. She's always been petite with short blonde hair worn in a bob and bright blue eyes. She looked very similar to Linda, the sister immediately above her in age, although Linda is taller and a bigger build. Bernie was laid back as a child and less outgoing than Linda, although she won't take any nonsense from anyone. Having said that, she's the type of person who loves everybody and wants everybody to love her. She can sing like the rest of us, but she's also turned into a terrific actress.

★　★　★

The aches and pains in my legs meanwhile persisted. They didn't really bother me when I was playing with my sisters or my friends but I'd complain about them at the end of the day. The way I used to describe them was like having a headache in my legs. Eventually it reached a point where it was decided I should be put into a sort of hospital so I could be observed more closely. It was called St

Gabriel's Convalescent Home in Cabenteely on the outskirts of Dublin, about an hour on the bus from where we lived. I never questioned what was happening. I was a child and it was adults who made decisions. I simply did as I was bid. Anyway, I was either told or I'd somehow worked out in my head that I was only going to be there for three days and then I'd be back home again. So I saw it as a bit of an adventure.

What also made it quite exciting was that Maureen was admitted at the same time as me. She'd been told she either had a high blood count or hypertension, whatever that may have meant. These days, she'd have been given some pills. Back then, though, I think it must have been the fashion to encourage bed rest in the hope that whatever was ailing you would go away. It was a bizarre way of dealing with any physical complaint, especially when it involved children. As it was, Maureen remained in Cabenteely for a year while I was there for an astonishing eighteen months, never once being allowed out to visit home. Because so many grownups were telling me it was for the best, I simply accepted the situation as my fate, never questioning it.

When Maureen and I first arrived, there was a measles epidemic, so the nuns said we had to stay in the convent with them. We were put in a room on our own. Mum used to come and visit us twice a week, Wednesday and Sunday without fail, when she'd bring us what was called our 'pigeon' — biscuits and little treats, kept in your own individual tin box.

I only found out much later on that, during our first two weeks in the home, there was a bus strike in Dublin. Mum never said anything but, unable to drive and not being able to afford taxis, she hitchhiked across the city. Dad would come with her on Sundays, but he was working in the week. When we had measles, visitors were only allowed to look at us through a glass window. They couldn't come into the room in case they carried in germs from outside. I know Mum found that hard and I remember crying each time she left.

At the start, Maureen and I were told to stay in bed almost all the time. We'd be seen by a doctor once a week who might say that we could get up for, say, half an hour a day. Then it went up to an hour a day and so on, but if we ever did anything wrong, we'd be told we had to revert to just half an hour a day. It was all very strange. I never felt remotely ill, even though there was a more or less continuous dull ache in both legs — although not always at the same time. And still no one seemed able to explain what the cause was.

Once the measles epidemic had passed, we were then put on different wards according to our ages. Maureen was only six and I know she found it hard not having her big sister with her. In time, we were allowed to do pretty much what we wanted. I'd get up in the morning and play with the other children, or help in the kitchen and then deliver meals to the other patients. There were only girls in the home, and most of them around the same age as me. There were about twenty girls on my ward, many of them with heart conditions but all expected to make a full recovery.

We'd listen to the radio a lot; Cliff Richard and Elvis Presley were very popular at the time. Or we'd play draughts or snakes and ladders, if it was winter and we had to stay indoors. In the summer, as long as the weather was nice, we'd be allowed out in the grounds where we'd play tig or hopscotch or skipping games.

We were taught by a teacher who came in each day, a mixture of lessons including maths and Gaelic which was as much a mystery to me then as it is now. I'd see Maureen at playtime but I was horrible to her. I'd run away from her saying, 'You're not my sister.' I deliberately tried to make her cry.

Then I'd go up to her and give her a cuddle and tell her I was only kidding, that I loved her really. I think I just wanted her to want me. So I'd goad her until she cried and came to me pleading, and then I'd hug her and make her smile and have the satisfaction of making her better again. I remember deliberately making my sisters cry when they were babies, just so that I could console them. It was a form, I suppose, of exercising control and I'm not in the least proud of it.

Although we were supervised, the staff were busy so we'd get up to all manner of mischief. I remember once borrowing knives from the kitchen and one of the other girls and I sat in the grounds scraping all the bark off a tree trunk. On another occasion, one of the other girls and I decided to run away. We weren't unhappy; we were doing it out of sheer devilment. After lights out, we grabbed our coats, climbed down the fire escape and made our way through the grounds and out of the main gates.

'And where do you think two young girls like you would be going at this time of night?'

The voice of the local bobby stopped us in our tracks about a hundred yards from the convalescent home.

'Dublin, Constable,' I answered with a bravado that I certainly wasn't feeling.

'Then I think you're going to have a long walk,' he replied, 'because you're on the road to Cork. Dublin is that way.' He waggled his thumb over his shoulder.

As a punishment, my friend and I were put on a side ward. There were only two beds in it and we had to stay put for a week, only permitted to get out of bed to go to the toilet. It was the isolation unit, screened off by glass from the main ward. I can't say it made me upset, just angry.

Of course I used to have the occasional bout of home-sickness during all this time, but I've always had the ability, even as a child, to rationalise these things. I wasn't going home in the foreseeable future so what was the point of wasting my emotions on wishing I could be back with my family?

I made my Confirmation in the convalescent home and Maureen made her First Communion. I was ten; she was seven. It was at about that time that I went to Lourdes. We had a neighbour in Raheny who worked for an organisation that sent sick people there, and Mum asked her to put my name on the list. However, my mother couldn't come with me. I was put on a stretcher and lifted on to a night train, sleeping in a couchette enshrouded by a privacy curtain. When the party got to

Lourdes, I stayed in a hostel with other young people. I was perfectly capable of walking although, on the occasion I was taken to the Basilica, I was placed in a wheelchair and pushed by one of the Boy Scouts. I didn't mind. I was an obedient child even though I was spirited, too. To be honest, I think I rather enjoyed the drama of it all. I remember it very clearly. There was a procession in the evening when hundreds of people carried candles down a hill to the village, an absolutely amazing event for a ten-year-old girl who'd been stuck in a home in Ireland. All you could see were candles in every direction. All you could hear was beautiful singing. Eventually, I was taken to the grotto, dressed in a special robe, and told to get out of my wheelchair and walk through a sunken stone bath filled with freezing water. At the other end, there was a statue of Our Lady. I was told to kiss her feet and, as I did so, I was dunked under the water. The strange thing was that, the moment I climbed out of the bath, I was completely dry in a matter of seconds.

My mother said she was convinced I was cured while I was there, but of what no one could rightly say. It occurs to me now that I could perfectly well have told the doctors in the convalescent home that the pains in my legs had stopped and then maybe I'd have been allowed home — but that wouldn't have been true. They ached in just the same way before, during and after my trip to Lourdes. Anyway, I wasn't desperately unhappy there, so why pull a stunt like that? Maybe, if I stayed a little longer, they'd discover what was causing the trouble and then I'd be cured and released.

There never was a convincing explanation and, to this day, I still get aches and pains, immediately below my knees.

★   ★   ★

In the summer of 1961, Mum made another trip to England and her enthusiasm for moving to Blackpool was reignited. Again, Dad was reticent. He loved Ireland. Why would he want to move to England? But then Fred Daly, who she'd met on her previous visit, decided to come over to Dublin to convince my father to change his mind.

Fred was the managing director of a company called Union Printers. He had no connection whatever with show business, but he'd heard Mum sing, and I think he was rather smitten, of course by her looks but especially by her voice. They were chatting afterwards and she told him all about my dad, and Fred was insistent that they should bring the family over to England. There was a huge network of clubs in the UK that simply didn't exist in Ireland. Fred was convinced they'd be a big success because there was a greater scope for the type of music my parents were singing.

He was tall and slim with a kind face and a nature to match. He was divorced when my mother first met him, although he did have a girlfriend at the time. He may have fancied Mum, but I also think he was genuinely struck by her talent and potential. I was later to grow very fond of Fred, giving him the honorary title of Uncle. He was very kind to me because, apart from my recurrent aching legs, I also suffered from blinding headaches and he would massage the side of my head until I fell asleep. He was a big supporter of Blackpool Football Club and he and my dad took me to my first football match, the start of a lifelong love affair with soccer.

Uncle Fred must have done a pretty good job of convincing my father that the family's future lay in England because the decision was made to move there in June 1962. He only had a three-bedroom semi, so it was a pretty unusual offer to encourage two adults and seven children to come and live with you. Actually, it was two adults and six children. I was still in the convalescent home — Maureen had just been discharged — and the doctors were not prepared to authorise my release.

My parents nonetheless decided to move without me. I remember the whole family coming to say goodbye. It was a very sunny day. And then they all left. I was usually accepting of my fate, but I did cry then. I felt so alone. Although I'd seen my brothers and sisters on my Confirmation in the convalescent home chapel, as well as on my birthday, I'd known that Maureen was on the next ward and that the rest of the family were returning to the home I knew and loved. But when they left to travel to England, I felt very flat. When would I see them again? And where? I couldn't imagine my mum making the long journey back to Cabenteely, just to see me. Whichever way I tried to rationalise it, it felt a bit like I was being abandoned. I remember being very tearful for the first couple of days after they'd said their goodbyes. But I was a tough, resilient little girl and, gradually, I rallied. I told myself that this had been a difficult decision made in my best interests. Also, somewhere deep in my heart, I knew that nothing lasts for ever. One day, although I didn't know when, the situation would be bound to change. Wouldn't it?

That was the June of 1962. I was eleven and I had no idea what the future held. When they'd discussed leaving, my parents were told that Maureen was fine, they could take her — but if they also took me, the doctors could not guarantee what would happen to me. It would be Mum and Dad's decision and on their own heads be it. That's why, they said, they didn't want to risk it. But it didn't stop them moving to England.

Now, as a mother myself, I find their decision to leave me in Ireland utterly incomprehensible. I know my mum found it a wrench, but she still agreed to it. Not so long ago, I spoke to my Aunt Teresa about being left behind and she said she'd told my mother that she thought it was disgusting. I was a little girl of eleven being abandoned by her whole family with just my mother's Aunt Lily to keep an eye on me. Lily did come and visit me and I loved her, but it felt so strange imagining my mum and dad and all my brothers and sisters living in another country in a house which I'd never seen and couldn't conjure up in my head.

Then, in the following October, without warning and just a month shy of my twelfth birthday, I was suddenly signed off. My mother put it down to my being cured at

Lourdes, although I felt exactly the same as I did before I went there. My condition hadn't changed one jot but the doctors said I could leave the convalescent home. Heaven knows why. Maybe they thought it would be more beneficial for me to be reunited with my family. If so, no explanation was ever given for my release. I went to stay with Aunt Lily for a couple of days before her husband Alfie, and their daughter Trudie, came with me on the boat to Holyhead. Almost as soon as I arrived in England, I went to the Victoria Hospital in Blackpool for a complete medical check-up — my heart, my blood, everything. Apart from the deep-seated murmur, they could find absolutely nothing wrong with me, an opinion that remains the same to this day.

I hadn't been out of the four walls of the convalescent home for a year and a half, never mind the unfamiliarity of finding myself in an alien country. The drive from Holyhead seemed to go on for ever through a landscape where everything looked strange and foreign. I tried concentrating on what was going on inside the car in an attempt to anchor myself to something — or someone — familiar. I remember laughing at Trudie while she repeatedly licked her fingers and wet her hair as she put in rollers. I'd never seen anything like it. As we eventually reached Preston, the huge volume of traffic was at a virtual standstill, something I hadn't encountered before. I was so naïve that, as we approached Blackpool, I was fully expecting to see an enormous black pool.

★　★　★

Uncle Fred's house was a redbrick semi and posher than where we'd lived on the Raheny estate in Dublin. It was in an area of Blackpool called Layton, some of which was quite smart and some a bit run-down. Uncle Fred's house was in the nicer bit. There was a small front garden and a little raised path leading to the front door. There were two living rooms downstairs and a long, narrow kitchen leading to a yard beyond. The three bedrooms were upstairs. One of them was Uncle Fred's, another was my parents' and Denise, Maureen, Linda, Bernie and I were all in the third. Tommy and Brian slept in the back lounge downstairs. There was also a bathroom and toilet.

The culture shock was acute. It was pandemonium.

On top of it all, it was odd being reunited with my brothers and sisters, very odd. Denise still tells a story about my mother saying to her something to the effect that she wouldn't be needed any more because I was coming home. She would no longer be the eldest daughter. What Mum meant was that Denise would be relieved of some of the duties of helping look after the little ones, but she was terribly hurt by this comment. That helped to explain, I think, why Denise seemed rather resentful of me when I got to Blackpool and was standoffish with me at first.

Generally speaking, my brothers and sisters seemed rather wild, all yapping and scrapping the whole time, almost like strangers to me for a while. They weren't mean to me, and they tried their hardest to include me, but I'd grown unused to the rough and tumble of family life and I'd missed out on so many shared experiences, especially those of Denise and Maureen, the two sisters closest to me. I was like a little mouse after all those months being shut away. My confidence had been sapped to the point where I almost didn't feel like one of the family. I felt very young for my age.

I realise now that I was shy in their company, which may be a funny thing to say about your own family but it was true. In time, though, I began to be rehabilitated back into family life. Activities that involved all of us were a real help. My dad was keen on

Monopoly, so we'd have evenings when the whole family would play. Or we'd all join in card games: Snap or Rummy or Whist, or something called Uno. He always had time for us all. Sometimes, we'd sit and listen as he read us stories from the Bible.

It was already the middle of the Christmas term, so everyone was at school, with the exception of Bernie who was still a toddler. For some reason, it was decided that I shouldn't start until the beginning of the new academic year the following September. It meant that I missed the first year of senior school, but maybe my parents were still concerned that I should be properly well again before I took on the demands of a full-time education in what was to me a foreign country. Not that I got any tuition from either of my parents in preparation for going to secondary school.

While I may have been timid to begin with, I was always strong beneath the surface and I started to come out of my shell. Soon I began to assert myself. On one occasion, we were in the park where there was a jazz swing, a large wooden plank that you could sit on as it swung back and forth. I was over the other side of the park on the swings. When I looked over to where Denise and Maureen had been playing, I saw a girl I didn't know ordering them off the jazz plank so that she could swing on it alone. I walked over and asked them what was going on. They pointed to the girl. 'She made us get off,' said Maureen.

I put my hand on the plank and stopped it from swinging. I turned to my sisters. 'Right,' I said, 'get back on.'

The girl said, 'No, they're not.'

I wouldn't back down. 'Yes, they are,' I said, 'and you're getting off.'

So she did and we had a fight. I pulled her hair and pushed her and knocked her glasses on to the ground. I picked them up, handed them back to her and then told her to push off. I'm not a naturally aggressive person, but I can't bear injustice, particularly when it comes to my own family. I'm a Scorpio, very loyal but with a sting in my tail.

I liked the weekends, and also when Denise, Maureen and Linda came home from school each weekday afternoon because they were company for me and we could play together, but the weekdays during term time dragged on endlessly. Between October 1962 when I arrived in Blackpool and the following September when I finally started at secondary school, I was stuck at home — at Uncle Fred's — every day. I'd do a bit of housework or watch TV or help look after Bernie. Mum had a job with a football pools company, but

Dad didn't work during the day. He relied on the money he made singing in the clubs at night. So it was just him and me and Bernadette who wasn't yet two. With the house to himself, Dad had free rein to do what he wanted.

And that's when it began.

3

The Ultimate Betrayal

What happened to me at the hands of my father remains crystal clear in my mind and yet I can't remember the first time he started touching me. I think I know the reason for that. I was eleven, just about to be twelve, and I knew nothing about sex. This was the early sixties and, if sex education was taught in some schools, it certainly hadn't been in the convalescent home. Nor was ours the sort of enlightened family where a subject like that was openly discussed. My mother never told us when she was pregnant and I have no recollection (with the exception of her last pregnancy with Coleen) of her changing shape.

Whether what I'm going to describe was the first time or not, I don't know, but it was certainly typical of what happened. I can remember being in Uncle Fred's kitchen. There was an open fire which was lit because it was winter. Dad was sitting on a chair. He pulled me towards him and sat me on his knee. That wasn't something he'd ever done before, as he wasn't a demonstrative man, but I can't say it rang any alarm bells in my head.

It was cosy in there and I thought my father was merely wanting me to curl up and have a little snooze. Everyone was still keeping an eye on me because of my medical history and because I was still getting aches and pains in my legs and I'd been told that I had some sort of a heart murmur. It seemed natural that I should be encouraged to take a rest during the day.

I relaxed against his body, my head tucked into the nape of his neck. He started stroking my hair with one hand and then he put his other hand between my legs. He was stroking me down there and saying soothing words. I wasn't sure what was going on, but I don't remember feeling awkward. He was being so reassuring, telling me how special I was to him. Then I remember him saying that, because I'd been away so long from the family, he wanted to do something nice for me. I trusted him. He was my dad. It must be OK. Maybe this was something other dads did with their daughters.

That's perhaps the wickedest aspect of it all: he played on my ignorance, my innocence. It's difficult to be precise about every detail of what went on because this was a journey on my part into uncharted territory.

I can remember the physical sensations he was unleashing in me, but I couldn't have any idea what was happening to his body. As an adult now, I can only assume that he must have had an erection because otherwise it wouldn't have made any sense, but, at the time, I didn't notice whether or not he'd become hard for the very good reason that I'd never seen a grown man naked. I wouldn't have known what happened to his penis when he was aroused. Also, he hadn't undone any of his clothing, so I couldn't see that part of his anatomy. However, on subsequent occasions, he began moving me around on his lap at the same time as stroking me between my legs, a pretty clear indication to me now that I was being used to bring him to orgasm.

My father didn't speak one word while this part was going on and nor did I. My overwhelming reaction was one of puzzlement. I remember thinking to myself: 'Why is Dad doing this?' He continued to gently move me back and forth in his lap, his hand still between my legs as his breathing became heavier. I wasn't frightened, just a bit confused. I didn't struggle to get away from him. I let him carry on and then, suddenly, without warning, he stopped. He lifted me off his knee and then got up and walked from the room without a word.

A couple of days later, it happened again and then the day after that. By now, I was beginning to feel the first unformed stirrings that this was something unnatural. It wasn't yet as strong as revulsion, for the good reason that I was ignorant about what was really happening, but buried somewhere deep in my subconscious mind was the dawning realisation that my father was doing something wrong. Why otherwise did I instinctively know to keep it a secret? Dad had never once asked me to. If I'd thought this was something that fathers and daughters often did together, I'd have mentioned it to my mum or I'd have asked Denise or Maureen whether he did it with them. But I told no one.

It didn't happen every day and, of course, never in the school holidays because all my brothers and sisters were in the house then, but when it was just my dad, me and Bernie, it was a fairly regular occurrence, almost every weekday by the end. And I began to enjoy it. It makes me feel so guilty having to admit that, but so angry, too. He never referred to it as such but my dad's 'special treat' started giving me a pleasant sensation. What a terrible violation of a vulnerable child! All that followed — and we had a fabulous career as the Nolans — is tainted by what he did to me. He killed stone dead the unquestioning love a daughter should feel for her father. I love my mum unconditionally. I feel nothing for my dad.

To this day, I'm convinced my mum knew nothing of any of this. I think it might have killed her if she had. She never once asked me any leading questions or dropped any sort of hint that she suspected something might be going on. If she did know and was in denial, she must have been an extremely accomplished actress. But my mum wasn't like that. Her emotions were always on the surface, which is why I'm sure — although I cannot, of course, prove it — that she was entirely unaware of the dark deed going on under her roof. I was never tempted to tell her, though. For a start, I was still getting to grips with whether something bad was happening. But this was all mixed up with a simultaneous feeling that somehow I should be feeling guilty about what my father was doing to me. It all seems clear cut enough now. But I was a child of twelve at the time and not a very sophisticated one at that.

There was never any penetrative sex, but abuse is abuse. This adult was bringing himself to orgasm — not that I understood what that was — day after day and using me, a naïve child, as the means to achieve it. Also, in time, he was bringing me to orgasm, too. I'm certain that was entirely incidental to him — he was only interested in his own pleasure — but to achieve that by masturbating your own child is unforgivable.

The routine never varied although he did sometimes try fondling my breasts, such as they were, but I never liked that and would push his hand away. I didn't say anything — neither of us ever spoke — but I do remember he laughed the first time he tried to do it. I didn't like that, which may explain my reaction, but, to this day, I don't really understand why I let him caress me between my legs but recoiled from the idea of him touching my breasts. He never kissed me, though.

My body must have got used to what was happening because I'd reach orgasm more and more quickly. My own father had awakened me sexually, a thought that still fills me with utter revulsion now that I can understand its full implications. He never hurt me, never slapped me around, but in some ways I wish now that he had, because that would have frightened me and I'd have known that what he was doing was wrong. I might even have said something to my mother. As it was, this was our little secret, an apparently gentle and loving act that seemed to please him and didn't upset me at the time. Only later was I able to see it for what it was.

In time, he started getting bolder. When he was moving me around on his lap, his breathing seemed to change; it was more urgent now and even heavier. That frightened me a bit and puzzled me, too. My dad had allowed me to think that he was giving me a pleasurable feeling. Was he getting pleasure out of it as well? If so, that didn't seem right, although in a way I couldn't quite articulate. I was gradually growing up and the doubts were starting to creep in. I began wondering why I made a point of deliberately not discussing what my dad was doing to me with anybody else. Why was I so determined to keep it quiet? Why wasn't I telling my mum that my dad was doing something to me that I really liked? Surely, that was some sort of subconscious recognition that this was a dirty thing? Slowly, the feeling began to take root that this was something we shouldn't be doing.

The memory of that game when the little group of seven-year-olds undressed for each other would come unbidden into my mind. I'd been told in no uncertain terms by my mother that what we'd been doing, however innocently, was wrong. I never saw my father naked, but by now he was putting his hand inside my knickers, stroking my vagina with his fingers. I'd learned from that childhood experience never to let anyone else see that private part of my body, not even my mother — and yet my dad was letting me think it was all right for him to put his fingers inside me. I was in turmoil. If Dad was doing what he was doing, it must be all right, I reasoned. He was my father. He loved me. But no, it couldn't be OK, could it? I remembered my mum had given me a good whacking for taking my clothes off and getting ready to parade naked in front of a little boy. These were called my private parts, she'd explained, and with good reason.

That childhood transgression, one that thousands of other children must have indulged in almost as a rite of passage, now assumed more significance than it might otherwise have done. What was my own father doing, touching me like that? I didn't have the definitive answer but, instinctively, I knew that this was worse than a childhood prank. Much, much worse.

Although my parents had no problem making babies, my impression was that theirs wasn't a particularly highly charged physical relationship, although I can't know what went on behind their bedroom door. I don't think my mother would ever have denied him sex — she adored my father — but it just wasn't in her nature to flirt with him in front of her own children, and Dad was much too enclosed, too buttoned up, to be so free with his feelings. However, for a long time I've had my suspicions that he was a serial adulterer. He had enough opportunity. He'd be away singing solo spots in clubs and I know women found him attractive. I'd seen that with my own eyes when I'd visited various clubs. They were always buzzing around him. Nor was he swatting them away. Given that he was prepared to pleasure himself using me as a means, I can't believe he didn't grab whatever chance presented itself for sex with anyone willing and available. Any female must have seemed fair game to him, but this is not something I can prove.

I want to think and hope that he never subjected any other young girls to what he put me through, but I have no way of knowing. I think he was slightly obsessed with me. I was his eldest daughter. I was the first to grow into a young woman before his eyes and under his roof. That doesn't for a moment excuse his actions, but it may go some way to explaining them. What it doesn't tell me is whether the incestuous acts that he performed on his twelve-year-old daughter meant that he was also a paedophile outside the home. Certainly, no whisper of that has ever reached my ears, but then, he was clearly able to keep his true nature hidden. In some ways, he was like two different people. He could be so warm and wonderful. He'd be the one we'd show our work to when we got back home from school. He was the one who'd taken us to the seaside at Bray when we were young and bought us fish and chips on the promenade. My mum was part of it all, too, but he took the initiative in all things. He was the boss, the one who ran the household. I might not have been comfortable with what had happened when we were alone together but he was still my dad.

Unlike most men of his generation, he would help bath the babies and change their nappies, and I truly don't believe there was any sick motive behind that. He was simply helping my mother and enjoying being part of family life. He drew the line at some things, though. It was Mum who used to do all the dirty work of going to the pawn shop when we lived in Dublin to get money to buy us shoes, and she was the one who'd scour the second-hand shops for clothes for us kids. We were poor because there were so many mouths to feed, although I can't honestly say I remember having a deprived childhood.

There was just never quite enough money to go round.

Later, he used to drink heavily — whisky and brandy were his favourite tipples — but, back then, he didn't have that excuse — if you can ever have an excuse for what he did, for molesting me. What he did, he did stone cold sober, and it seemed to be an almost daily requirement of his during that period when he had me to himself. I still have so much pent-up anger about what he did. To this day, I hate him for making me feel guilty when I discovered the true implications of his actions, but, thinking logically, I tell myself that I didn't know any better and that it was a nice feeling, which is why, in my innocence, I didn't try to stop him.

That period of almost a year in Uncle Fred's house, before I started attending secondary school, was when I was subjected to a barely broken time of sexual abuse. Once I began school, nothing was ever like that again, mainly because my father simply didn't have the opportunity. But that didn't mean he stopped trying.

I don't know how he could look at me and, more especially, at himself after he'd done the things he did. It was as if he could put the parts of his life in separate compartments. I distinctly remember we were all watching a programme on child abuse on the television. 'How on earth can people do something like that?' he said. 'It's just plain disgusting.'

And I was thinking, 'Am I making this all up? Am I dreaming?' But I knew I wasn't making any of this up. I knew I wasn't dreaming.

I still don't understand how I could have kept my silence about everything my father had done to me. Part of the explanation, I suppose, is that I was frightened of how he'd react. I didn't fear physical violence at his hands — that wasn't his way — but he was a powerful and persuasive man. Who was going to believe this teenage girl when he dismissed, as I knew he would, my accusations as mere fantasy? Anyway, if I'd endured months and months of sexual abuse in Uncle Fred's house, why had I never said anything to anyone? It would have made no sense. The fundamental reason why I protected my father's grubby secret was that I was scared of him.

I was terribly unhappy and unable, however foolish that may sound, to find a release for my unhappiness by unburdening myself on anyone else: my mother, my Aunt Teresa, one of my sisters, a friend. So I tried as hard as I knew how to fill my mind with positive thoughts. They didn't entirely obliterate what had happened — how could they?

— but it is possible to separate different aspects of your life. Otherwise, you'd go mad. That didn't mean I found it easy to deal with; it was particularly hard when I was on my own or lying in bed at night, turning it all over in my mind.

My mum was out at work during the day and my father was singing most evenings, so it was rare to see them together. If they were, she'd be busy doing things — cooking or cleaning or washing or getting the little ones ready for bed — while my dad would be watching TV. There was very little obvious interaction between the two of them. They dealt with the day-to-day demands of keeping a large family together, but there was precious little time left over, even if they'd been inclined, to sit around and chew the cud.

Certainly, if my distress was apparent to my father, he didn't show it. None of this seemed to be bothering him. Perhaps he just didn't care. Or perhaps he was an undiagnosed schizophrenic. He appeared, in fact, to be in complete denial, a man with the ability, apparently, to blot out anything inconvenient from his mind. He made the bold statement, for example, about the paedophiles paraded on television.

He was reacting as any normal person

would react except both he and I knew he wasn't normal. He couldn't have been to abuse me day after day, month after month, whenever the opportunity had presented itself. Because I knew what he'd done to me, I always felt a tension between us, but he seemed to be able to carry on a perfectly normal coexistence with my mother. I never heard them quarrelling or even bickering. Part of the reason for that, of course, was that she always deferred to him, bolstering his view that he was the head of the household. This suited my father, a man who liked to be in control.

Once we'd moved from Uncle Fred's, that attitude extended to our lives beyond our own front door. From the time we'd all moved to Blackpool, boyfriends had been off the agenda as far as he was concerned. He'd always claim that it wasn't us he didn't trust; it was the boys. If word got back to him — usually via one of my younger sisters — that I'd been seen talking to a boy, I wouldn't be allowed out for a week. He wouldn't scream and shout, but his face would be like thunder and then he'd denounce me in front of the rest of the family.

'You're no better than a tart,' he'd say, and then he'd ostracise me.

That meant he would deliberately not address a single comment to me until he considered I'd learned my lesson. He could ignore me for anything up to three weeks. He just blanked me, so I did the same back to him. To be honest, I found it embarrassing. He was behaving to me almost as though I was his wife or his girlfriend and we'd had the equivalent of a lovers' tiff. But I was his daughter; and he was an adult. It was a strange, inappropriate way for him to behave. It wasn't natural. My younger sisters got the same treatment in time, but less frequently and less pronounced. I always felt I was the pioneer in anything to do with my father because I was his eldest daughter.

If he was talking to me, and we disagreed about something, he'd turn to whoever else was around. 'Oh, Anne won't agree with me,' he'd say, 'because she hates me.' This was pretty accurate, as it turned out. 'If I say something's white, Anne will say it's black.'

He knew perfectly well the reason why, of course, but he could never admit it. What surprises me, looking back, is that no one else in the family picked up on our antagonistic relationship. You'd have thought my mother might have been curious about it, but she never said anything. My father was in charge and she wasn't about to question his behaviour. Later, as I moved into my teens, when things got too much for me, maybe once, possibly twice, a month, I'd go and stay with Aunt Teresa. I never told her what was happening at home and she never asked. I just needed to get away. I'm sure my mother didn't like me doing that. I could sense she was a bit hurt that I'd prefer to be with her younger sister but, typically, she never said anything.

If only I could turn back the clock, and have had the courage not to keep his dark secret to myself. My mum would have been shattered, although I wouldn't have properly understood that at the time because I didn't yet realise the full depravity of his actions, but just a chance remark about Dad stroking me down there would have put a stop to everything. Then I wouldn't have had this lifelong cloud following me around. However, a mixture of embarrassment and guilt somehow combined to hold me back.

I'd long ago made the decision to tell no one what my father had done to me when we were alone together. I still didn't properly understand the full ramifications of it but I was increasingly sure that it was a bad thing and a bad thing, moreover, of which I had been a part. By this stage, anyway, the school holidays were approaching so there'd be lots of people in the house and my dad would never be alone with me. After that, I'd be going to school every day.

★ ★ ★

I remember starting at that secondary school and feeling very vulnerable. I was put in a class where everyone else seemed to know each other. They were laughing and joking; I felt a complete outsider, the new kid with the Irish accent who didn't know a soul. Some of the girls would mimic the way I spoke, which I hated. Then Denise came across a girl called Jacqui who was also new to the school and, it turned out, was in the same class as me, so she approached this girl and told her about me. It was the best thing she could have done.

They used to call me Little John and Jacqui Friar Tuck. I was tall and skinny; she was small and a bit chubby. She had dark hair, dark eyes, pale skin, just the same as me. She was an extrovert, but not in an overbearing way. We were a week apart in age. There was an immediate bond between us: she didn't know a soul in the school and nor did I; each of us was naturally a bit apprehensive. It was inevitable that we'd start going around together, but it was more than that: we clicked. To this day, she remains one of my closest friends. But I was never tempted to tell her my secret. By then, I was pretty sure what had happened was wrong so I was worried she might think that I was in some way to blame. I never told anybody because the older I got, the more ashamed I became.

Jacqui and I would talk, as girls do, about the facts of life, or our sketchy understanding of them, at least. There was a girl in our class who got pregnant at fourteen, a real scandal back then, and I remember discussing with Jacqui how babies were made. A lot of it was guesswork. We hadn't a clue about the sexual act. Certainly, we never discussed masturbation. We simply had no knowledge of it — ironic when I realised later that I'd been involved in exactly that without really being aware of it. I never, ever said a word to Jacqui about what my dad had been doing, but, over those weeks and months chatting to my new schoolfriend, there was a dawning realisation in my mind that his fondling of me was sexual. And totally wrong.

As that knowledge strengthened, I felt a mixture of horror that it had happened in the first place, shame that I had allowed it to happen (albeit innocently) and anger that my own father had done that to me. The more I understood the full implications of his actions, the more this swirl of emotions intensified. There was also the sad acknowledgement that the father I'd known when I was nine and we were all living in Dublin no longer existed. He'd been destroyed and it was his fault alone. Our relationship had gone beyond the point of no return.

Jacqui was always there for me. She knew what my dad was like, without ever being aware of the fact that he'd been sexually abusing me. I'd always be complaining about him. There'd be some sort of club activity after school and I'd tell Jacqui I couldn't come to it because my father wouldn't let me. Or she'd ask me to go to the cinema and, nine times out of ten, he'd say that I couldn't.

I think now that he wanted to keep me as his little girl. He wouldn't allow me to wear tights to school, for instance. He insisted I continue to wear socks. We'd sometimes have parties at school in the evening, but I was never allowed to stay out later than nine o'clock, and, because I always had to leave early, Jacqui started getting friendlier with a girl called Joan. I didn't blame her, but that didn't stop me minding. I liked Joan, too, and a girl called Patsy, but Jacqui was my best friend.

It was Jacqui who gave me my first bra. My mother was of that generation too embarrassed to talk about how your body changed when you hit puberty. A lot of mothers back then were like that. A friend of mine thought she was bleeding to death when her periods started. No one had told her what to expect. We did have some sort of guidance at school about menstruation but, even so, I had no idea how to cope when it happened to me soon after I started secondary school. I asked my mother and she handed me an old stocking and a pad. I was meant to thread the stocking through the loops of the pad and then tie it round my waist. It took me years to get the hang of tampons, not least because I was too shy to ask for help.

Years later, when Jacqui was living in Wigan with her husband, she came to see us perform in a club there. She was pregnant with her first baby. My father announced her from the stage.

'Look at her,' he said, 'that's Anne's best friend. Before the mark of the cradle's off her backside, she's pregnant.'

Jacqui, quite rightly, was really upset. 'What do you mean?' she said. 'I've been married two years.'

My father's attitude to sex seemed to be that it was all right for him wherever and with whoever he chose, but it was something to be derided in young women.

When I think of my father now, part of me just feels dead, part of me still feels real anger. One of the saddest legacies of being sexually abused is the ball and chain of guilt you drag around after yourself for ever afterwards. There might be some satisfaction, I suppose, if I were somehow able to explain to him the effect of what he did to me, but, in the end, I suspect it would have offered scant comfort. Those things happened.

I refuse to feel bitterness, a wasted emotion that does no more than eat you up, and I can't write him off as a monster, even if some of his actions could only be described as monstrous, but neither can I lightly brush aside the way he exploited my innocence for his own perverted gratification. Sadly, some children suffer far worse sexual abuse than I ever knew, but there is no league table for this sort of thing. Once a man can see his own daughter as a sexual object, he crosses a line from beyond which there is no way back. And, anyway, the abuse isn't only physical, not for the victim, at least.

My father may have invaded my body, but he also invaded my mind. I'm now in my late fifties, and yet, to this day, no recollection of my childhood can ever be carefree, and that includes the years before the abuse began. It has a contaminating effect that seeps into every corner of your mind, every facet of your life. It doesn't go away, and the slate can never be wiped clean.

4

Suffer the Little Children

In 1964, when I was thirteen, my parents bought their first house. When we moved to Waterloo Road from Uncle Fred's, I didn't like it. It was bigger than his place, but it was a bit run-down, and dark and dingy, too. In time, however, Mum and Dad paid for somebody to knock down a wall to combine a couple of rooms downstairs and repaint and decorate the whole place.

The house was terraced. There was a long hall with a staircase leading up to the bedrooms. Immediately on the left as you came through the front door, there was a front room, kept for best. I remember the first time that Jacqui came to the house, she and I were allowed to eat in that room on our own. My dad had set up a table for us. At the end of the hall, there was another family room and a kitchen with a yard off it where there was an outside toilet that had been converted into a coal shed.

Immediately in front of you as you came up the stairs, there was a box room at the back of the house where my two brothers slept. Then there was a combined bathroom and toilet on the left-hand side at the top of the stairwell. A left turn up three or four steps would take you to three bedrooms. In the first, there were two sets of bunk beds: Maureen was on the top of one and I was on the bottom; Denise was on the top of the other with no one beneath her. Linda and Bernie were in the front bedroom. And my dad was in the second small box room.

I never thought about why my parents didn't sleep in the same bedroom; maybe they didn't want any more babies. My mother slept on a couch downstairs. I know she had to get up very early each morning to light the fire, to make our breakfast and to get us off to school before she herself went to work: perhaps she felt she'd disturb fewer people by sleeping on the ground floor.

Our next-door neighbours were called the Flecks, Ena and Neil. She had three children, Alan, Linda and Suzanne Gallagher, from her first marriage; Suzanne was my sister Linda's best friend. Then there were Mark and Joanna by Neil.

Mrs Fleck was a Scot, a lovely woman with a very distinctive, quirky sense of humour. She might ask one of us to go to the local shop for her and get her a cabbage 'as big as your head'. She was a real joker. I remember telling her once that there was a cigarette butt stuck to the sole of her shoe. 'Oh, I know,' she said. 'That's where I keep them.' Later on, we'd get back from a gig at one or two in the morning and she'd make bacon butties for all of us. You couldn't have wished for a nicer neighbour. She was fabulous. I'm still in touch with her to this day.

Because our house wasn't centrally heated, there were always wet knickers hanging all over the fireplace to dry while everyone would fight for a central position in front of the fire. And because the toilet was in the bathroom and because there were so many females in the house, my brothers used to have to nip next door to Mrs Fleck's, if they needed to use the loo. Or, if she wasn't at home, they'd have to go up the road to the public toilets on the corner.

Being part of a large family was fun but I loved going to school or to stay with my lovely Aunt Teresa. I got on well with my brothers and sisters and my mum, too, but I was always cautious around my father. Since I'd started school, no opportunities had presented themselves for him to molest me again, but that didn't mean I wasn't wary in his presence. Who knew when he might strike again? As it happens, I didn't have to wait long to find out.

One night, I woke up with another of my fierce headaches and went into my dad's room. I was groggy from sleep, my head was pounding, I think I was a bit disorientated. I just headed for the nearest parent, without thinking. I wanted something to ease the pain. Dad went off, returned with some headache pills and then said, 'Get in beside me.'

I wasn't at all sure. 'No,' I said, 'I don't want to. I'll go back to my own bed.'

But he was insistent. 'You've got a bad headache,' he reasoned, 'you'll keep the others awake. Much better if you sleep here.'

He had a huge amount of natural authority and I wasn't about to cause a noisy scene with everyone else in the house sound asleep. So, reluctantly, I did as he told me. It was a single bed. He was by the wall; I was on the outer edge. I lay on my back for ages before eventually falling asleep. The next thing I knew, it was early morning and the sun was streaming through the curtains. My dad was still asleep.

As I pulled the bedclothes back, my hand brushed across my nightdress — and a wet, sticky patch. Then I felt something resting against my stomach. It was my father's penis. I recoiled in horror. Without thinking, I moved it away, got out of bed and ran to the bathroom where I scrubbed and scrubbed myself in an attempt to feel clean again. I was in a daze, and yet I felt I had no one to confide in. I knew I could never tell another living soul the unbelievably disgusting truth: my own father had masturbated over me, his own daughter, while I lay sleeping.

It was such a shock, truly the worst thing he'd ever done to me. I felt dirty, degraded, debased — and totally betrayed. Stupidly, I'd trusted him when I wasn't feeling well, and this was the contempt with which he'd treated me. I'd gone to my father for help. Here was his response. If there had been any last small hope of repairing our fractured relationship, that single filthy act had put a stop to it once and for all.

I never willingly went anywhere near the man again. If we were ever alone in the same room, I'd position myself as far away from him as possible. From that day forward, I wouldn't sit next to him on the sofa if we were all watching television. I couldn't bear the thought of him even touching me. Not that you'd ever have guessed what he'd done to me from his demeanour or behaviour. There wasn't even a tacit acknowledgement of the disgusting things he'd done.

And still I wasn't entirely safe from my father's dark desires. I remember the night, not too long after, when Dad arrived home drunk after performing in a local club. I heard him climb the stairs and walk unsteadily to the bedroom I shared with Denise and Maureen. He came over to where I was lying and put his hand under my bedclothes, fumbling to fondle me between my legs.

Immediately, I sat bolt upright.

'Stop it!' I hissed under my breath. 'I don't like it.'

He simply laughed, the smell of alcohol on his breath hot and rank on my face.

'Don't! Get away!' I was almost shouting now. I pushed him as hard as I could. It wasn't difficult because he was so wobbly on his feet. I was grinding my teeth in fury. Again, he just laughed at me and stumbled out of the room — but it must have made some sort of impression: he never, ever tried to touch me between my legs again.

Even allowing for all of this, my life wasn't one of relentless domestic gloom and abuse. Christmas, for example, was always a magical time. We'd get up and go to Mass and then there'd be a marathon session of opening all our presents which would last for hours. Mum would cook a late breakfast and she'd be in charge of Christmas dinner, although my dad would help her. That would start around four o'clock.

When we'd finished the traditional meal of turkey with all the trimmings, we'd tuck into my mother's homemade Christmas pudding, the best I've ever tasted, before or since. We'd stay at the table for anything up to four hours, eating and laughing and drinking and singing a mixture of carols and seasonal songs. Our favourite was 'Have Yourself A Merry Little Christmas' which we sang in five-part harmony. Friends and family would come round later on and we'd play games.

Good times weren't confined to Christmas, and I remember when we'd sit in front of the big coal fire at weekends during winter and have a good laugh watching a movie on TV on a Saturday night. We were all particularly keen on westerns, for some reason. My dad used to give us money to go out and buy sweets first at the corner shop. However, I never loved that house or those days like I loved the time in Raheny in Dublin. Little wonder. My life had changed by then. Now, I was a wary girl on the cusp of becoming a young woman who didn't feel comfortable sitting next to her own father on the family sofa.

★　★　★

When it came to the first stirrings of our semi-professional career, the landscape was much brighter. In Blackpool alone, there must have been at least twenty working men's clubs that offered entertainment every night, so there was no shortage of opportunities for my parents to find singing engagements, both separately and together.

Denise had quickly become keen on putting on little 'concerts' in the garage of the house on Waterloo Road. She'd rope all of us in and my friend, Jacqui, too. Then Mum and Dad as well as various friends and neighbours would have to pay sixpence each to come and see a performance. We'd sing songs from *The Sound of Music*, Denise having taught us the harmonies. None of us ever had any lessons, but all of us had a good ear, all of us could sing in tune. It's an ability, I suppose, we must have inherited naturally from the gene pool.

I had been raised in a musical family and been singing, just for the fun of it, for as long as I could remember. Apart from those little shows Denise put on in our garage, I'd never performed professionally, though. All that began to change when Tommy was thirteen and I was twelve. Our parents took us both to the British Legion Club in Blackpool one evening when they had a booking there, and at one stage during their act, they introduced us to the audience and we sang a couple of songs along with them.

Denise and the rest of us used to pester our parents to take us with them when they went off to sing in the clubs. That's how it all started really. We'd be taken, just one at a time, to whichever club it was and Mum and Dad would allow us to sing one song for the audience. I remember I liked doing 'Moon River' which I'd sung at a talent contest Aunt Teresa had taken me to not long after I joined the rest of the family in Blackpool. I hadn't known it was a talent contest. She just told me to get up and sing so I did, and I won. I loved performing — we all did, I think — and I can't ever remember being nervous. In fact, I liked the feeling that singing in public gave me, but I wasn't really conscious of the audience or of their applause at the end. I was in my own little bubble.

I enjoyed the working men's clubs. There wasn't anything like them in Ireland and they seemed so full of life. They were always noisy and smoky, but I never minded that; it just added to the atmosphere. It was a treat if our parents said we could go with them. They'd buy us soft drinks and crisps and we were allowed to play bingo. It all seemed so exciting.

In time, they'd sometimes take Denise and Maureen as well. We loved it and so did the audience who always responded enthusiastically. As a result, our appearances with our parents became more and more frequent and it wasn't long before we'd evolved into a family act: my mother and father, two brothers and us five girls — even little Bernie. We became known as the Singing Nolans.

We'd sing songs like 'Beg, Steal or Borrow' that had been made famous by The New Seekers and that we'd heard on the radio, as well as songs from musicals. I'd sing the melody, Denise would do the high harmony and Maureen the low one.

We'd do three forty-minute spots in the evening accompanied by our organist Roly Haworth, with Tommy on drums. In the intervals everyone would play bingo or there'd be a raffle. When we finished our third spot around 10.30, we'd get taken home either in my dad's car or by taxi. We might do as many as four nights a week, singing in one club or another. We didn't get paid at this stage, although we always got pocket money if we asked to buy comics or sweets. If we weren't performing but Mum and Dad were, Tommy and I were considered old enough to look after ourselves and the little ones at home.

We never rehearsed and there were no routines to learn first thing in the morning, which we'd read was how The Osmonds were put through their paces by their father. It was only later that the hours became ridiculous and we'd miss school because we were so tired. At this early stage, though, it was all innocent fun, even if I do remember resenting sometimes having to go to sing with my parents when I'd have preferred to be out with my friends.

Our popularity grew. News of us spread quickly, and as it travelled further, so did we. People would come and visit Blackpool on holiday or for the nightlife and they'd come and see us perform. When they returned to their homes, we'd start getting bookings in other towns and cities. There's nothing more effective than word of mouth. Gradually, we were travelling to south Wales, to Scotland, the Midlands.

We were all still at school, but that didn't stop us. We'd often travel for two or three hours to a gig, do our three sets and then have to turn round and come home again, often not getting to bed until three or four in the morning. Then there'd be school just a few hours later.

I distinctly remember Mum coming into our bedroom. She'd shove each of us awake.

'Come on,' she'd say, 'it's time to get up for school.'

We'd moan and groan that we were too tired. She'd go downstairs to see to the food and stoke the fire, then we'd be disturbed from our slumbers again.

'Come on,' she'd shout up the stairs. 'You're going to be late! You're going to be late!' Throughout all of this, of course, my father was dead to the world, asleep in his bed in the box room. If they ever discussed the fact we were burning the candle at both ends, I certainly never heard it. Our household didn't operate like that. We weren't a family for sitting around debating what we did. We just got on and did it. I can't recall a single occasion when I eavesdropped on my parents discussing what was best for us children. Dad would say that something was going to happen. Mum would try and make sure whatever it was did indeed happen. And that was that.

Rising from our warm beds was tough enough in summers but winters were worse. The house had no central heating in those days. Mum, poor thing, would have been out of *her* bed an hour before anyone else to set the coal fire in the lounge where we'd eventually gather, half asleep, to eat breakfast, assuming, of course, that we'd managed to drag ourselves from our beds in the first place. Some days, we'd get to school late; some days, we didn't show up at all. And as for homework . . . I rarely did mine because there wasn't time and anyway I was too tired. I can clearly remember trying to scribble as much as possible in my exercise books on the bus to school.

It's gone now, but St Catherine's Roman Catholic School for Girls was very well respected with a particularly good reputation for music. The head teacher, a nun called Mother Bernard Joseph, was very strict, but I thought she was fabulous. I loved her. I was a member of the choir which was one of the best school choirs in the country. The choir mistress, Margaret Holden, was a cousin of Margaret Thatcher's. She liked me, I think, but later on, when she realised how often I was singing in local working men's clubs with my parents and some of my siblings, she was very disapproving. Denise was in the choir with me as well as Jacqui and my other friends, Patsy and Joan.

On one occasion, we were due to sing at the Albert Hall, and we had to be at Talbot Square in Blackpool at six in the morning for the coach trip to London. Denise and I hadn't been to choir practice the night before because we'd been singing in some club with

81

Mum and Dad. My mother had got up at five o'clock to make us sandwiches and then we went off to catch the coach. We'd just sat down when Margaret Holden signalled to us to come and have a word with her.

'Where do you two think you're going, Miss Nolan?' she asked. She had a rather sarcastic way of talking.

'The festival, Miss Holden,' I replied. 'We're going to London.'

'No you're not,' she said. 'You didn't come to rehearsal yesterday evening so you're not going to London today.' And she made us get off the coach and go home. It seemed such a mean thing to do. I hated her, but not for stopping us going to London; a bit of me understood the reason why. I hated her for not having told us the day beforehand. She shouldn't have waited until we'd got up early, all excited, and made our way to the coach. Both Denise and I were bitterly upset. We ran home in tears to tell our mum who was very philosophical. 'She's obviously not a very nice person,' she said. 'Just forget it.' But it was hard on us.

This was no way for a child to be educated and now, as a mother myself, I feel genuinely shocked that my parents could encourage such a way of life. We children loved appearing in the clubs, loved the adulation of

82

the audience. But what did we know? It was like asking a child to ration the amount of sweets she ate. That's why adults are given the responsibility of judging what's best for a child.

My father wasn't interested in any of that — and, make no mistake, he was the one who was in the driving seat. He could see how well we were going down in the clubs and he wasn't interested if our schoolwork and our physical wellbeing were shot to pieces as a result. My mother might have said something but she didn't. From the start, she'd been cast in the role of obedient wife.

The teaching staff took a dim view of our increasing professional singing engagements and it's not hard to see why. One of the teachers wrote on Maureen's report that her nightlife would leave her 'permanently retarded' which seems a bit over the top. I enjoyed school, but it made me anxious that I was always behind with my homework. Letters would arrive at home about our poor attendance record, and comments would always be made on our end-of-term reports. My dad would read them and then simply ignore them.

It's little wonder that I never sat a GCE exam, despite being a potentially capable student. In the event, I left school at the end of the summer term in 1965, some four months before my fifteenth birthday, and without a single qualification to my name. It never occurred to me to stay on. I was singing in clubs regularly by then. It was clear that this was going to be the path I was destined to follow — and happily too. Demand was growing for appearances by the Singing Nolans. Wherever we sang, people would turn up in their hundreds to see us. We'd walk past the queue snaking round the block as we arrived at a succession of clubs and people would be clamouring for our autographs. There was never an empty seat and we never left the stage without a standing ovation. It was intoxicating stuff and infinitely more exciting than getting down to our schoolwork. We loved singing and the public seemed to pick up on our enthusiasm.

Our main attraction, I think, was that we were all members of one family. Audiences, young and old alike, were intrigued and seemed to respond to that. Some people liked us for our own sake, but others came to reinforce their view that *their* family could do what we were doing. That almost certainly wasn't true. Each and every one of us could sing confidently in tune which is why we all had our own solo spots in the act. Some fans would come to every single one of our performances and a few of them became our friends. I particularly remember a couple called Marlene and Graham Collins who'd often help by driving us home with our stage wear at the end of an evening. When I was a bit older, they'd also take me all over the country to watch football matches, one of my favourite pursuits.

I lapped it all up, loving the warmth of the applause, but, even so, I felt torn in two. Because I was in my teens, I longed to be with my friends, going to discos, staying over and having girlie nights. So, much as I enjoyed performing, I resented it, too. I hated missing out on all the normal things a teenager enjoys doing and that included going out with boys. My friends were getting boyfriends; I was singing. I'd send Jacqui postcards from everywhere we went if we were performing away from Blackpool. We'd be working sometimes as many as five nights a week, so it was very hard to keep our friendship going.

At the same time, Dad was becoming obsessive if he caught us even looking at a boy in the audience. It started when I was thirteen, so Denise can only have been twelve and Maureen ten or eleven. Just one glance from any of us in the direction of a boy while we were performing and he'd be on at us when we came off stage. His reaction was always the same.

'I saw you flirting with that boy,' he'd say. 'Still, if you want to act like a little slut, that's up to you.' He'd be sneering, sarcastic rather than shouting the odds.

I ignored him, deliberately refusing to answer back, but that didn't stop me thinking that perhaps he truly was mad. Did he seriously imagine that his daughters were going to remain spinsters until they died? Or was it that he somehow wanted all of us for himself? The result of this irrational behaviour, of course, was to make me as secretive as I knew how. If I saw a boy I liked the look of, or ever got chatting to one, my father would be the last person on earth I'd talk to about it.

It sickens me to this day to think that he was telling me I was making myself look cheap by, at the most, glancing at a boy, when he'd done the things he'd done to me. Even though I'd shown him in the most forceful way I knew how that I didn't want him touching me or getting anywhere near me again, he'd still try it on when I was least expecting it. I was in the kitchen in Waterloo Road on one occasion — I must have been fifteen by now — filling the teapot with boiling water from the kettle just before we were due to leave for another singing engagement. Dad came into the room, walked up behind me and reached out in an attempt to touch my breasts.

I wheeled round on him. 'Go away!' I shouted. 'Leave me alone.'

He laughed, in a way, I think, that was meant to make me believe he was just having a bit of fun. 'I've told you,' I said, 'just go away.' But he made another lunge at me. I had the teapot in one hand, the kettle in the other. As I jumped and tried to push him away, the boiling water spilt all over my hand. My piercing scream brought my mother running into the kitchen from the lounge to discover me shocked and trying to stifle my sobs from the pain.

'What on earth's going on?' she asked, crossing the room to see why I was so distressed.

'Dad was fooling around,' I said, 'and he knocked my arm when I was filling the teapot with boiling water.' Even though my hand really hurt, my instinctive reaction had been to cover up for my father. He was the picture of innocence, of course. He butted in and pretended that it had all been no more than a bit of horseplay and that I didn't seem able to take a joke.

What I should have said was that Dad had

been trying to fondle my breasts. But I didn't. This was an opportunity for me to tell my mother everything that had happened between my father and me, but, once again, I didn't speak up and tell the truth. In a way I was covering for him and I still don't really know why, perhaps partly because I felt embarrassed that my father would want to do something like that to his own daughter. I placed my scalding hand under the cold tap and said nothing. Then we went off to whichever club it was, my hand still throbbing. I placed it against the cold car window to try and ease the pain, my father in complete denial, acting as though nothing had happened.

5

Walking on Eggshells

Because I was no longer at school, I'd sometimes get up and light the fire before the younger kids went off in the morning, allowing my mother to have a bit of a lie-in. Mostly, however, all the household duties fell to her, although my father would help a bit. He'd do the vacuuming without being asked and he was quite practical. He liked everything to be tidy, and yet he'd have piles of papers, all stacked neatly, which he'd leave on the kitchen table or somewhere that drove my mother mad. She'd move them because she was trying to get the dinner ready and then he'd be in a thunderous mood all day.

He was the manager who handled all our bookings and he couldn't bear it if his paperwork was disturbed in any way. Although we were attracting more and more local bookings, we never had much money in those days. A big family like ours took a lot of feeding and clothing, and then, of course, there was our stage wear. To save money,

89

these outfits were made by my mother and Aunt Teresa.

I recall long, emerald green pinafore dresses worn over white blouses which we'd always wear if we were singing an Irish medley. Then we had costumes like the kids in *The Sound of Music*, with scarves on our heads. Mini-skirts were fashionable then, so we also had short sequinned dresses worn above the knee. We might work the same club twice a month, so that would mean new outfits that hadn't been seen there before.

I remember once arriving at a club and we'd forgotten our little white socks which we girls always wore on stage. We were horrified to think we'd look like waifs and strays without them. Luckily, by the time we were due to perform that evening's second set, our cousin Sandra had arrived with white socks all round. I look back now and they seemed, in many ways, such innocent days.

By now, my father had started drinking quite heavily, although not during the day. I'd say he was a borderline alcoholic. I still don't know why his drinking increased. He wasn't under any pressure that I knew of. I think it may have been no more than the fact that he could afford it and he enjoyed the taste of alcohol. I always knew if he was drunk — we all did — because he'd get a strange white mark at the side of his mouth. He'd start getting sarcastic or dismissive, both of which I shrugged off.

But the thing that frightened me was when he'd then drive us all home. As our fame began to spread beyond Blackpool, so we'd gradually have to travel further afield for singing engagements — and then face the long journey home, my father at the wheel and in no fit state to be driving. The breathalyser had not yet come into force. There could be as many as six or seven children in the car, and we were clearly a major accident waiting to happen, but somehow he never crashed.

My mother couldn't drive, but we did have a friend, John Quinn, who'd occasionally drive us as a favour. John worked during the day and I know that he didn't always want to go off driving in the evenings, but my father had a way of making people do what he wanted — and, in this case, for no fee. He had a very persuasive, powerful personality.

In contrast to all these far-flung gigs, we were engaged to appear for a summer season at the Brunswick Club in Blackpool for nine consecutive years, throughout my teens and beyond. That meant six nights a week, two or three shows a night, from July until the illuminations were turned off at the end of

October. We filled the club night after night, although my younger sisters — Linda and Bernie — had to be off-stage by nine each evening; that was the law of the land. Technically, we all had to have a licence to perform in public under the age of sixteen, but no one ever seemed to enforce it for Denise, Maureen and me.

During those seasons at the Brunswick, Dad liked to stay behind after the show and prop up the bar. Because we lived close by, we kids were usually sent home by taxi, albeit much too late for our age, and promptly put to bed. Later, I'd hear Dad returning, stumbling into the house, and I'd lie rigid in my bed in case he came into the bedroom I shared with Denise, Maureen and Linda. It was driving home from the Brunswick late one night that my father had stopped the car and told me he wanted to say something special.

That episode haunts me to this day. As soon as he'd said that he'd give me a lift home, I'd felt uneasy, but nothing could have prepared me for his obscene suggestion that we should run away and live together as man and wife. The abuse I'd suffered at his hands had been bad enough, but this was worse. I remember being gripped by a new panic. Was this an overture to our having full sex together somewhere that very evening? It was late. It was dark. He could have driven me anywhere and easily have overpowered me. My tears, my abject fear, must have communicated to him, though, because he had suddenly started up the engine and we'd driven straight home, in silence.

The thought of him blundering drunkenly into my bedroom and trying to grope me was a real and constant fear with his increasing drinking. It was worse if Blackpool FC were playing at home, although any trouble usually occurred in the evening rather than during the night. He'd go to the match and arrive home considerably the worse for wear before we invariably all had to go off for a singing engagement. That's when he'd pick a fight with Mum. She was the very opposite of a belligerent woman, but he'd go on and on at her until she was goaded into reacting.

Every Saturday, she'd make a big pan of stew from which we could all go and serve ourselves at whatever time suited us best. By the time my father got back from the football match and the drinks afterwards, all the stew would be gone. He'd march into the kitchen.

'There's only potatoes and vegetables left in this stew,' he'd say. 'Where's all the meat?'

My mother would try and keep calm. She'd

say, 'It's not my fault, Tommy. The kids must have eaten it all.'

That would never satisfy him. 'You know how many of us there are,' he'd reply, in a really patronising way. 'Why don't you put more meat in the stew in the first place?'

And so it would escalate until she said something like, 'Well, if you didn't stay out drinking, there'd be plenty of meat for you.' Then he'd smack her one, a slap across the face. Or he'd push her across the room. He never cared if any of us was there. Fuelled by alcohol, he no longer kept a lid on his naturally bullying nature.

The truth is, anything she said would have set him off, and he'd carry on riling her, determined to pick a fight. I'd beg her over and over again to say nothing when he came through the front door with the drink on him, but it was no good. He'd needle her, she'd eventually answer back and then there'd be trouble.

One night, just before we set off for the Brunswick, Dad came back from the football, drunk again, and a row started between him and Mum. I'd seen it so many times before. The three of us were in the lounge. For no good reason, he suddenly lashed out at her, as he'd done many times in the past. He slapped her across the face and then pushed her hard on to the sofa. She was trying to defend herself and crying now. I hated witnessing such violence against my poor mother, but she always told us to keep out of it. For some reason, this time it was different. All the simmering rage I felt about him, and what he'd put me through, boiled to the surface. I was really angry. He was hitting my mum and in front of me. How dare he! I wasn't going to stand by and let this continue. I knew exactly what I was going to do. I walked across the room and grabbed the phone.

'If you touch my mum once more,' I screamed, 'I'm going to call the police.'

He turned and fixed me with an icy stare. 'Put that phone down,' he said, his voice suddenly cold and measured, 'or you'll get the same treatment.'

I wasn't going to be intimidated. I screamed my warning for a second time.

Dad marched across the room, snatched the phone from my hand and punched me full in the face. It wasn't a slap. It was a blow from the closed fist of a grown man. I was so angry, so fired up, that I felt nothing except pure defiance.

'Go on then,' I screamed through my tears, 'if it makes you feel like a man.' And he struck me again and again. I shouted at him, 'I don't care. You're not hurting me.'

He stepped back and looked directly at me. 'In that case,' he said, 'I'll make you care.' And he slapped me so hard across the face, it split my lip. This might have been the moment when I blurted out the disgusting things I'd suffered at his altogether less violent hands, but I was only concentrating on the here and now. Dad was out of control. Mum was hysterical.

'Leave her alone!' she shouted, over and over, as she did her best to try and pull him off me, but he was too strong for her and anyway deaf to her entreaties as he struck me repeatedly across my face.

Then, for no reason I could understand, he abruptly stopped. Just like that. Suddenly, it was business as usual. We were due on stage for our first set within the hour. Nursing my bruised and swollen lips, split and bleeding from my father's repeated slaps and punches, I tried to pull myself together for that night's three performances.

What really upset me was my mother's reaction. After my father had left the room and gone into the kitchen, Mum came up to me. 'You shouldn't have interfered,' she said as I clutched at my face. 'You only made it worse.' What she should have been doing was denouncing my father, but she never, ever did. I remember feeling angry that she hadn't thanked me for sticking up for her. But I could never be cross with her for long.

My biggest concern was that I mustn't let my brother see what had happened to me. 'Don't tell Tommy,' I implored my sisters. 'Please don't tell Tommy.' They'd been upstairs getting ready during my father's outburst, but Tommy had been out for the day with his mates and was joining us at the gig. If he knew that Dad had lost it, all hell would break loose. Things were bad enough as it was. I couldn't bear the thought of them getting any worse. I just prayed he wouldn't see the state of my face beneath all the make-up.

As soon as I got to the club with my sisters, however, he could tell I was avoiding him in the dressing room.

'What's the matter with you?' he said.

'It's nothing,' I lied. 'I tripped.'

He looked me square in the eye. 'Dad did that, didn't he?' he said. 'I'll fucking kill him.'

I said, 'Oh, Tommy, please don't make it any worse. It's all done with now. For my sake, please don't do anything.' And he respected my wishes. I just didn't want any more upset to do with my father. Anyway, we were due on stage so there wasn't time to discuss what had happened.

Tommy's relationship with our father was

becoming more and more combative. He was growing into a young man and he was wanting to assert himself. He was really getting into hard rock music, which my dad hated, and he'd started wearing his hair long and seldom brushed, his clothes casual; in other words, he was the complete opposite of how my father presented himself. I knew all of this irritated Dad who'd always been opinionated to the point of not wanting to hear anyone else's view on anything. For instance, Sinatra was king; hard rock was rubbish. End of story. He'd say to Tommy, 'Anyone who likes heavy metal must be an idiot.' And then that would be the start of another argument.

'You can't tell me what to like,' Tommy would say, 'and just because you don't like it doesn't mean it's not any good. I'll listen to what I want.'

'Not in my house, you won't,' my father would reply, but Tommy would take no notice.

On one occasion I'd been staying overnight at Aunt Teresa's when my brother Brian suddenly turned up at her house, looking really worried. Tommy and Dad had had another of their rows, but this time it had got physical. They'd had a proper, full-on fight, wrestling and punching each other. Tommy was seventeen by now and perfectly capable of taking on my father. Brian wanted me to come home and keep the peace, so I did as he asked, but, by the time I got there, the row had blown over and Tommy had gone out.

These days, you'd call my father a control freak, and he hated having to acknowledge that his elder son was no longer at his beck and call, but he made sure that his wife was under his thumb. One of the ways he controlled her was through money. I remember one particular Christmas Eve when I was in my mid-teens. Mum still hadn't been out and bought the turkey or any of the trimmings for the Christmas dinner because my father wouldn't give her any money. She was crying and pleading. 'Oh, Tommy,' she said, 'if I don't go now, the shops will shut and then we'll have nothing to eat tomorrow.' He'd been out drinking and he was playing with her, taunting her, deliberately withholding the cash she needed.

'I'll give it to you when I'm ready,' he said, smirking all over his face.

He was the one who controlled the purse strings. My mother always had to ask for money to buy anything. In many households, the man would hand over his pay packet and his wife would give him back a bit of beer money. Not in ours. I never saw her do this, but I assume she must have given him her wages from working at the football pools company. It meant going cap in hand to my father if she had to buy food, or clothes for us kids, or anything. He'd give her whatever he judged to be the right amount on each occasion, but that depended in turn on what mood he was in.

★   ★   ★

When it came to the act, though, Dad was becoming a bit more relaxed, more or less leaving us alone in terms of what we chose to sing. No one was more in charge than anyone else. We were each allowed to pick our individual songs which we sang as solo spots between the group numbers.

I'd do a Karen Carpenter song or 'As Time Goes By' from the film *Casablanca* or 'I Understand' which had been a recent hit for Freddie and the Dreamers. Denise would sing a big power ballad, something dramatic which suited her style and her personality. Maureen sang Nancy Sinatra's 'These Boots Were Made For Walking'. Brian might tackle a Sinatra song, while Linda, who couldn't have been much more than seven, got kitted out in a slinky dress to sing Shirley Bassey's 'Big Spender'. Even Bernie, then aged about four, would put on a cloth cap and sing 'Strollin'' or 'Show Me The Way To Go Home'. We all enjoyed singing — nobody was made to do it against their will — so what was the harm? That, at least, was our attitude at the time.

Word of our success spread and we'd get bookings even further afield. We'd all pile into Dad's estate car — it was replaced in time by a minibus — and sleep all the way there and all the way back. I remember one occasion, driving over the Pennines in the snow, when the windscreen wipers packed up. Quick as a flash, Mum whipped off her stockings and tied one to each wiper. Then we had to take it in turns to sit with one arm out of the window yanking the stockings back and forth so that Dad could see where he was driving. It was a bitterly cold night, but somehow we made it home in one piece. I don't remember anyone going to school the next day, though.

By now, we were being booked by bigger clubs which could hold anything up to three hundred people so, if we got three or four of those in a row, we could afford to live quite well. We might clear a thousand pounds in a good week, a fair bit of money back then. There wasn't any left over, though, what with the cost of material for our stage outfits, petrol bills, Dad's drink and all those mouths to feed. But we didn't go short.

We started to build up an incredibly loyal fan base, some of them young men who'd talk to us between shows and ask to take us out. I remember in Wigan being chatted up by two lads who obviously fancied me and Maureen. They'd always come and see us whenever we went back there and they also came to Blackpool. Neither my sister nor I fancied either of them, so my father had nothing to worry about. On one of those gigs in Wigan, we got invited back to the house of a family who were among our most ardent fans. They were so keen for us to have a quick cup of tea before starting our journey home, we felt we couldn't refuse. While we were there, my mum happened to admire their dining room table.

'Then take it with you,' said the woman whose house it was.

'Don't be silly,' said Mum. 'We can't just walk out of here with your dining room table.'

'Of course you can,' she said. 'We've just bought a new one, so we don't have any more use for that. We'd love you to have it.'

Before long, we were back on the road, the table lashed to the roof rack of the estate car — but none too securely, as it transpired. About halfway home, the table shook loose and shot off the roof, landing upright in the middle of the road. Linda and Bernie were whimpering in the back, frightened that something would happen to Dad as he went to retrieve it. But he came to no harm and we completed the remainder of the journey, sitting round the table in the back of the estate, my father having lowered the car seats.

★   ★   ★

I was fourteen when Coleen was born in March 1965. I was so embarrassed about my mother being pregnant, I didn't like to talk about it to anyone. It must have meant that she and my father had had sex which I couldn't bring myself to think about, partly because no child likes to think of their parents doing that and partly because of what he'd done to me.

I loved Coleen from the start, and when I left school she spent most of her time with me. Initially, she slept in a drawer in a cupboard because there wasn't a cot for her. Then she slept in my bed. I still smile at the memory of this sweet little girl sitting in the middle of the floor fast asleep in the early hours of the morning as I remade the bed she'd wet, a habit she's long since grown out of (as far as I know!). My mum was at work all day again, so I became Coleen's sort of surrogate mother. She almost seemed like my baby.

Most teenagers, as they head towards their twenties, are beginning to make their own way in the world, but my father remained in my life far longer because of the stage act. I remember we used to sing 'Somethin' Stupid', the song made famous by Frank and Nancy Sinatra. I'd sing one half with my dad, then Denise would sing the second half before all three of us sang the finale. I used to hate that song. Dad made me feel that he really meant the words he was singing. He'd look deep into my eyes as he sang, 'And then I go and spoil it all by saying somethin' stupid like I love you.' I wouldn't meet his gaze, and I didn't feel comfortable singing the words 'I love you' back to him because I didn't. He'd ruined our relationship and there was no way back. It felt like I no longer had a proper father.

Apart from pouring scorn on our musical tastes — The Beatles were dismissed as rubbish, for example — he'd also criticise us for the way we spoke. This was the sixties so I'd use words like fab and groovy. 'Why do you want to talk like that?' he'd sneer. He'd also undermine our confidence when it came to singing, but he'd do it insidiously, picking us off one by one.

I remember saying to him on one occasion, 'Can I sing a solo sometime, Dad?' He told me I could, so I practised singing 'I Understand', but each performance came and went and my father never let me sing it. On the one hand, he was letting us choose our favourite songs for our individual solo spots, but then he couldn't resist flexing his muscles if the mood took him and, what's more, he'd do so in as unkind a way as he could.

I asked him if I could sing 'I Understand' on a specific evening, just before we went on stage. 'No you can't,' he said. 'You always sing flat.' I've never forgotten that. It simply wasn't true, but it was the kind of thing he'd say every so often. Brian still hero-worshipped Dad at this stage and he tried to sing in the same style. My father would sometimes praise him for that but, on one occasion, he turned on him and said, 'You'll never be able to sing like me.' It cut Brian to the quick. Like all bullies, Dad would belittle you with spiteful barbs which made you doubt your ability and which perpetuated his sense of control over you.

I'd lie in bed and dream about running away from home so I could escape his clutches, in every sense of the word. I'd talk about it with Jacqui, and we'd fantasise about

105

living in London together, but I never once mentioned to her anything about the sexual abuse. I wouldn't have run away though, because I'd have been too scared. Anyway, I'd have missed my brothers and sisters too much, as well as my mum.

Because there were so many of us and because we both lived and performed together, we were self-sufficient. Of course we all had our friends outside the family, but we also had all these home-grown friends, too. No, the sole reason for leaving home would have been to get away from my dad. I just didn't want to be around him. Sometimes, I'd fall asleep wishing that when I woke up the next morning he'd be dead.

As I grew older, he continued to keep a beady eye open for any boys showing what he considered to be too much attention. In 1970, the Singing Nolans — that was the entire family including Mum and Dad and all eight children — were booked to perform on a cruise for two weeks in the Mediterranean. I was twenty and Maureen was seventeen, and we met a couple of sailors we liked. I even secretly kissed the one I fancied — they were both called Dave. They said they'd come and visit us in Blackpool the next time they got shore leave — and that's exactly what happened.

We told everyone where we were going and who we were going to meet, with the exception of my father. He was out singing, but we knew we had to be home by 10.30 that night. As we neared the house, Brian was waiting at the gate with my mother.

'Quick! Quick!' he called. 'Dad's on his way home.' Brian had always idolised my father and never wanted to be associated with anything of which he'd disapprove. We broke into a sprint, abandoning the Two Daves who'd been strolling down the road with us. We ran up to our bedroom and there was a broom in my bed and a mop in Maureen's, put there by Mum and Brian to look as if we were fast asleep under the covers. We threw them out of our bunks and dived in fully clothed.

I think back to that incident now and it seems barely believable. I was a young woman. I should have been able to stay out all night if I'd wanted, but nobody liked to do anything that would upset my father, me included. The man had an aura about him which is difficult to explain unless you were one of his children.

He never laid a finger on us in anger when he was sober, and yet we were all fearful of what might happen if we disobeyed him in some way. For one man to have the ability to strike fear into the hearts of an entire family of nine, and to do so without having to resort to habitual violence, says much about the strength of his personality.

If ever I contemplated my future, therefore, it isn't perhaps too surprising that I found it hard to get past the point of getting out from under my father's influence. How, and when, would I be free? I just didn't know. I felt trapped in a tunnel and there didn't seem to be even a glimmer of light at its end.

In the meantime, life had fallen into a familiar pattern. We'd do a season at the Brunswick every summer, and for the rest of the year we'd be booked by a wide variety of clubs, mostly in Wales, the north and north-west and Scotland, although occasionally we'd travel down to London, usually for a corporate event. In 1971, the Singing Nolans won the Clubland Act of the Year and appeared at the Empress Ballroom in the Winter Gardens, Blackpool, to receive our award.

Audiences were unfailingly enthusiastic and we even recorded our first album, a collection of the songs we sang in our stage act. It wasn't a sophisticated production even by contemporary standards, the only instrumental backing being piano, bass and drums, and no opportunity either for doing retakes.

The cover picture was taken in Stanley Park near where we lived. Never mind, the object of the exercise was for the Singing Nolans to have an album to sell in the clubs — and sell it did, hand over fist.

But now we kids were getting restless. We were popular, but really only in working men's clubs. Month followed month, year in, year out. It was as though we were stuck in a bit of a professional whirlpool. We wanted more. We wanted to be on television. We wanted to be famous. We idolised The Osmonds. Might we ever have even a fraction of their fame? Despite our best efforts, the right break seemed to be eluding us. It looked as if it was never going to happen.

★ ★ ★

I was washing myself in the bath one day — I'd have been twenty-two at the time — and, although I never went in for self-examination, I was surprised to find a lump at the top of my right breast. My GP referred me to the hospital and a specialist there said I'd need to have an operation to remove the lump — or mouse, as it was referred to, because it moved around.

It turned out to be quite large; I needed thirteen stitches after they'd cut it out. I was so naïve, it never occurred to me to ask if there could be anything sinister going on. I remember being released the next day and my chest was swathed in a large white bandage. A couple of weeks later, we were doing a gig and I went to lift the boot lid of the car to put the cases in. My mother scolded me. 'Don't do that!' she said. 'You've just had an operation.' I ignored her and of course the stitches burst, reopening the wound in my breast. The legacy to this day is a crescent-shaped scar.

Two weeks later, I had another hospital appointment to hear the results of the tests they'd run. The doctor asked me to sit down and then said, 'I'm happy to tell you the lump's benign.' I looked at him blankly because I didn't know what he was talking about. 'Well, it's not cancerous,' he explained, the first time the possibility had ever crossed my mind. So I went back home, told my parents everything was fine and then forgot all about it. That wasn't hard to do because my life — and the lives of my sisters — was about to change for ever. It was Christmas, 1973.

6

Sister Act

Mum's jaw dropped as she stared at my dad.

'You've got to be joking, Tommy,' she said. 'Christmas? We never work at Christmas.'

He shook his head. 'I know,' he said, 'but the money's good and we can't afford to turn it down. Anyway, at least it's local.'

Mum couldn't argue with that. The Cliffs Hotel on Blackpool's north promenade, apart from being no more than ten minutes down the road, was also one of the most prestigious venues in town, although that was irrelevant. If Dad said we'd be singing there on Christmas Day — never mind that this was traditionally a time for celebration and family get-togethers — then that's what we'd be doing. There were a few grumbles among us kids but there was little point complaining. My father ruled the roost and it was easier in the long run to go along with what he said, rather than risk one of his silent moods.

So we climbed into our glad rags and, as with every performance, gave it our best. The audience was in festive mood and our

111

lunchtime show was warmly received. As we left the stage, Dad headed off to the bar and we made our way to a table reserved for the performers and waited for him to return with the drinks. He seemed to be taking longer than usual and, when he finally did rejoin us, he looked thoughtful, preoccupied. He distributed the drinks and then sat down next to Mum.

She knew instinctively that something was up. 'What's the matter, Tommy?' she asked. 'What's on your mind?'

He didn't say anything for a bit. Then he leaned closer to her and started speaking in little more than a whisper. 'Don't make it obvious,' he said, 'but there's a family to your left, three tables away. The man is small with dark hair . . . '

Mum looked in the direction Dad had indicated and nodded. 'Well,' she said, 'what about him?'

'He just collared me at the bar. His name's Joe Lewis. Says he owns some clubs in London and wants us to go there and work for him.'

Mum laughed. 'A gig in London? That'll cost him.'

'Not a gig, Maureen,' said Dad. 'Permanent. He's offering us a week to see how it works out. Then, if it's successful, he'll be

112

looking at a contract for something in the order of five or six years.'

My parents were conducting their conversation in such hushed tones that I was having to strain to catch what they were saying. Denise nudged me. 'Something's happening,' she said. 'What's going on?'

I told her to be quiet. 'I don't know yet,' I said. 'Something to do with London.'

Mum was talking again. 'What did you tell him?' she asked.

'I told him I needed to think about it,' said Dad. 'He gave me his phone number. I said I'd ring him with a decision soon.'

It wasn't until later that day, when we were sitting round the kitchen table having eaten our Christmas dinner, that we were all told exactly what was on offer. Dad explained as much as he knew about Joe Lewis and what he'd said. Joe had been immensely impressed with our performance, and had been particularly taken with the fact that we were a genuine family act. He was the boss of a company called Hanover Grand which owned, among much else, three function rooms and a restaurant in London. There was the Cockney, near Trafalgar Square, which could best be described as a sing-along with a meal, the performers dressed as Pearly Kings and Queens, dancing and singing songs about

London's East End. The Beefeater was similar with the staff dressed accordingly. The London Room, however, was much more classy, catering for an altogether more upmarket, wealthy, international clientele. A theatre restaurant, it was in the heart of the capital's West End. Finally, there was Verrey's, a long-established restaurant on Regent Street.

Dad didn't look very happy. 'I don't want to go,' he announced, with some finality. Once he was settled somewhere, he never liked to uproot. He hadn't wanted to move from Ireland to England. Now he didn't want to leave Blackpool for London. He was a man who didn't like change.

'Neither do I,' said my brother Tommy. 'I like living in Blackpool. All my friends are here.' Brian sided with his brother.

Then Maureen piped up. 'Well, I want to go.'

'Me too,' I said.

The discussion went round and round and on and on for what seemed like hours. In the end, it became clear that we five girls were standing firm against the men. This was the chance we'd been looking for and we weren't about to pass it up in a hurry. We were going to London, with or without the others. It was the biggest decision we'd ever made that flew in the face of our father's wishes, but we were tiring of the sameness of our lives playing the club circuit. We could sense that our careers were about to go up a notch and we weren't going to let that opportunity pass.

It was finally decided that Tommy and Brian would stay in Blackpool in the house in Waterloo Road; they were old enough to look after themselves. Tommy was twenty-four and had a job in the accounts department of a builders' merchant; in the evenings, he worked at the Brunswick as the club's resident drummer. Brian, who was nineteen by then, worked for another building firm, as a merchandising clerk. Each of them had girlfriends by this time too. Coleen was only eight and still at school so she'd live with our Aunt Teresa. She was perfectly happy with that, not least because she could never be parted, she said, from the pony my parents had bought her. Horse-mad from almost the moment she could walk, she loved to help muck out at the local stables, her favourite pastime in the world.

Mum was dead set on moving with us to London, even though it meant going against my father's wishes. I think she was fundamentally more adventurous than him. She was the one, after all, who'd first suggested trying our luck in Blackpool's clubs. Now, she was being beckoned by the bright lights of London.

Dad continued to dither, although he did eventually agree to join us a couple of months later. I think he felt that, as the head of the family, it was a massive undertaking to move all of us to somewhere like London and all on the say-so of one man. By contrast, Denise, Maureen, Linda, Bernie and I were young — I was twenty-three, Denise was twenty-one, Maureen eighteen, Linda fourteen and Bernie twelve — and we were certain. We wanted to be famous. We couldn't wait to start our new adventure.

The Nolan Sisters had just been born.

We weren't entirely unfamiliar with London. On a number of occasions, we'd been invited to do the cabaret at corporate events and we'd performed in the Great Room at Grosvenor House at an event called the Showman's Guild, the society for fairground people. We'd also sung at the Royal Garden Hotel in Kensington, again at a corporate event. In fact, that had been the first time we'd been to a big London hotel and we hadn't known what to expect. So naïve were we that we took our own portable TV in an old sewing machine case tied up with string. We must have looked like the Beverly Hillbillies. It had never occurred to any of us

116

that each room would have its own television!

When we first moved to London, us five eldest girls and Mum, we stayed in a miserable bed and breakfast just off Shaftesbury Avenue. It was near the underground so the whole place would shake every time a tube train rumbled by. London seemed fast and scary and awe-inspiring all at once; I hated it and I loved it. At the beginning, in any free time, we behaved like tourists. We'd go to Hyde Park or London Zoo or shopping in Carnaby Street.

Denise, Maureen and I shared a bedroom. We'd been there about a week when I decided to eat a few squares of chocolate before getting into bed at the end of another long day. I was dimly aware during the night of faint rustling sounds which were explained in the cold light of the following morning by the nibble marks in what remained of the chocolate bar. That was it. None of us was going to share a room with a family of mice or, worse still, rats. As the eldest, I marched up to Joe Lewis as soon as we got to the London Room later that afternoon. 'You've got more chance of spending the night with Mother Superior,' I told him, 'than of any of us sleeping in that rat-infested B&B ever again.'

He smiled. 'You can come and stay with

me,' he said. 'I've got a big house with plenty of space.'

You can say that again. Joe lived in a mansion that backed on to Wentworth golf course in Surrey. Suddenly, we were living in the very lap of luxury. I loved it, although my four sisters felt a bit out of their depth. They couldn't relax, they said, because it didn't feel like their home. They wanted the whole family to be together again.

Although Joe was estranged from his Irish wife, Esther, she lived under the same roof with their two children, Vivienne and Charles. I always thought Joe had a bit of a crush on me. He must have been about forty, a small man, not much taller than five foot, with dark-rimmed glasses. He took me out to dinner once or twice and he put his whole house at my disposal. He never made a pass at me, never tried to kiss me, but I got the feeling he'd like to if I encouraged him.

I was in seventh heaven at Joe's. I'd swim in the heated pool each day and then play tennis with Charlie on the private court in the garden. We girls lived there for a few months in the summer of 1974 while my mother commuted back and forth to Blackpool where Dad was still living and searched for a house near London where we could all be reunited. In the end, Joe Lewis, or one of his employees at Hanover Grand found a house in Ilford which my parents bought.

I wasn't in any hurry to move in. I was enjoying the liberation which came from being my own boss for a change. My sisters moved into Ilford before the work on the house was completed, but I stayed on in Wentworth until it was ready. By this stage, my dad had agreed to become the singer with the band at the London Room. He could tell that we were settled and happy and he liked the idea of coming to a guaranteed job. He'd perform after we'd done the cabaret, though Mum never sang in London. I think she was too busy looking after us girls.

Now, we five girls and Mum and Dad were all living together again. The Ilford house was fabulous, although I never once regarded it as home. That was Waterloo Road in Blackpool. The Essex house was double-fronted and detached with a steep set of steps leading to the front door. There was a small room on the right-hand side as you came in that was used as an office by my father and a secretary he employed called Elaine. He'd handle the financial side of the Nolan Sisters and deal with any fan mail. Also on the ground floor was a toilet, a dining room, a large lounge, a kitchen, a utility room and a bar at the back which we called Flanagan's after the Old

English sheepdog my father bought shortly after moving south. My dad drank much less all the time we were living in London. There seemed to be something about the club culture in Blackpool that encouraged his drinking but, even there, he wouldn't drink at home, only when he was out, and particularly after football matches.

There was a big garden full of apple trees and a swing. If the weather was bad, the washing would be hung in the enormous basement. On the upstairs floor, Denise, Maureen and I still shared a bedroom. Linda and Bernie were in another room and my parents had a bedroom each. I have to assume that the physical side of their relationship was now a thing of the past. In time, my cousin, Angie Breslin, the second eldest daughter of my mum's brother Charlie, came to live with us when she moved from Ireland to take up a job in the beauty hall at Selfridges. She shared a room with Linda Gallagher, our next-door neighbour from Blackpool, who'd also got a job in Selfridges, as a hairdresser.

★ ★ ★

For the first time in our lives, we were getting a regular wage: £120 a week to spend on what we liked. It seemed like a fortune, but then Joe was an immensely wealthy man with huge influence in all the right circles. We turned up for work one day and he introduced us to Stewart Morris, a highly respected television producer and Head of Light Entertainment at the BBC. He came straight to the point.

'I've seen your act, girls,' said Stewart, 'and it lacks polish. Your patter needs to sharpen up and I think your harmonies could do with some help, but, if we get all that right, we may be able to make stars of you yet.' Here was a man at the top of his profession telling us that he thought we had potential, so we weren't offended by some of his remarks. I'm sure there were plenty of rough edges that needed smoothing. The prospect was incredibly exciting, but we weren't nervous; we'd always been secure in the knowledge that we were all good singers with strong, individual voices.

Good as his word, Stewart introduced us to Alyn Ainsworth, musical director for the BBC and the man whose orchestra had often backed the likes of Shirley Bassey. Although our natural ability to harmonise had been at the root of our success in the northern working men's clubs, those harmonies, in truth, were far from sophisticated. We five girls would go to Alyn's fabulous apartment

121

in Chelsea where he'd teach us to harmonise intricately, producing a sound we could scarcely believe we were capable of making.

Then there was our appearance. All our stage clothes were now to be made for us by professional dressmakers employed by the BBC. Some of the outfits were fantastic: we all loved the sharp white trouser suits with diamanté trim and the initials NS picked out in red on the breast pocket, made by a talented Irishwoman called Jo Quill. On the other hand, we were also obliged to wear floor-length yellow dresses which we hated because they made us look and feel middle-aged. Platform soles were popular then, and I still marvel that we were able to execute complicated choreographed steps — we were taught by a man called Lud Romano — without falling flat on our faces. Off-duty, we dressed like any other young women at the time in jeans and T-shirts. We only ever wore make-up on stage.

We sang at the London Room six nights a week. When we finished each evening, the three eldest of us, along with Linda Gallagher and our cousin Angie, would go out on the town, often to the Valbonne, a club that was popular at the time, followed by the Candy Box which stayed open till seven in the morning. We'd eat breakfast at Mike's Diner off Regent Street before heading back to Ilford, sleep all day and then do the whole thing all over again.

Linda and Bernie, who were fifteen and thirteen by now, needed a special licence to perform because they were minors and still meant to be keeping up with their schoolwork. They attended a college in Ilford, just round the corner from where we lived, but they were burning the candle at both ends and I'm not sure their school attendance record would have stood up to too much close scrutiny. Whichever way you looked at it, it was a totally unsuitable life for girls of their age, but I don't ever remember our parents putting up any sort of objection.

There was one occasion when we'd been rehearsing with Alyn Ainsworth and, on our way back to Ilford, we decided to go into a Wimpy for something to eat. There was a group of lads at a table near ours and they started being cheeky, calling out things like, 'Fancy a good time, darling?' We ignored them but, while we were finishing our meal, I leant forward and whispered as softly as I could to my sisters, 'When I say run, run.'

Without the boys seeing what I was doing, I rolled up our sheets of rehearsal music as tightly as possible and then we stood up. As I passed by the lads, I whacked one of them as hard as I could across the back of his head and screamed, 'Run!' The boys came thundering after us, but gave up the chase when we reached the tube station. That's not something I'd dream of doing if I were that age again today. I'd worry they might be carrying knives — or worse.

Life was fun and the move to London had subtly but significantly altered my relationship with my father. He was never going to have a special place in my heart — what he'd inflicted on me ensured that — but he was no longer such an influence on our lives, a situation that he seemed to accept. He acted as our manager, but he never performed with us. The world had moved on and he accepted his new background role, both professionally and personally. I was in my mid-twenties and he must have known he could no longer tell me what to do, nor did he ever make any sort of inappropriate moves on me.

★　★　★

One of Stewart Morris's TV productions was Cliff Richard's hugely popular Saturday evening BBC series. At the London Room one day, Stewart told us we had to be on top form that night because Cliff himself was coming in specifically to see our act. There

124

was a new TV series at the planning stage and Cliff was looking for someone to fill the guest spot every show for six weeks. We couldn't believe our ears. Now we were nervous; we knew national television exposure on this level would elevate us to the big time.

Cliff had always been a pin-up of mine. All those years ago, when I spent eighteen months in the convalescent home in Ireland, I'd listened to his records all the time. He duly turned up that evening but, contrary to our expectations, he was far from being quiet and demure, whistling and calling out during our act. At one point, he threw his napkin on the floor, an indication, apparently, that he was really enjoying himself. Our performance over, we were invited to join him at his table. We were star-struck and tongue-tied, too. We let him do most of the talking. He didn't bother with any preliminaries. 'I'm impressed, girls,' he said. 'I thought you were terrific. In fact, I loved every minute of your act, and you're all pretty, too.' He paused. 'Well, how about it? What would you say to a regular guest spot on my new TV series?'

Would a starving cat refuse a bowl of cream?

The offer was confirmed a few days later with an official invitation from the BBC to appear each week on Cliff's show. He was lovely — kind, considerate, encouraging — and we all really liked him. However, we were terribly nervous. This was such a major development in our career. We'd be beamed into millions of homes every Saturday. We couldn't afford to let ourselves down.

The most terrifying part of it was that every song was choreographed. We'd only started learning to dance since landing the residency at the London Room. That was hard enough, but now we were expected to keep up to the mark with the Young Generation dance group sitting around watching us struggle through our rehearsals. They were lovely to us, though. Nigel Lythgoe was one of the dancers. He went on to bigger things, of course, as head of Light Entertainment at ITV and as a *Popstars* judge, before making his name in America producing *American Idol*. Bernie took to the dancing the best of all of us, Denise the least.

Every week, we'd sing a song on our own and then duet with Cliff. I remember we were all sitting in the lounge at Aunt Teresa's house in Blackpool to watch the first show in the series. We'd never seen ourselves perform before, never seen ourselves on television. You imagine it's going to be a thrill, but it's tremendously disconcerting. Suddenly, there you are as other people must see you. It's such a strange experience. For a start what struck me was that our outfits were grotesque. We were wearing full-length, bottle-green, satin dresses with long, silly sleeves, completely inappropriate for young women our age. Bernie was only fifteen and yet she was dressed like a middle-aged aunt. But, if you closed your eyes, we made quite a reasonable sound. Up until this point, we'd always sung what I'd call baby harmonies, simple stuff that we made up ourselves. Not on Cliff's show. Now, Alyn Ainsworth had taught us two- and three-part harmonies for each song. I even thought we moved quite well but, looking back now, it all seems so cheesy. The critics never said we were horrible or that our singing was hopeless; the bad press was always directed at how we looked, and that was more or less out of our control. We wanted to turn round and say that this image was one that had been created for us, that it wasn't how we were in real life. If you read the papers, you'd have imagined that we were whiter than white. On the other hand, all the coverage was making us famous; we were recognised in the street all the time now. And there are worse fates than being branded as virginal.

The great thrill for us at the time — apart from suddenly getting this invaluable national exposure — was that we met and worked with some of the top names in the business. The Three Degrees were major stars and they were on the show one week. So were Lulu and Elton John. They'd never come across us before, but they were all incredibly friendly and encouraging. I particularly remember Olivia Newton-John who couldn't have been nicer to us. She particularly hit it off with Maureen. Almost the next day, the phone rang.

'It's for you, Maureen,' I called.

She took the receiver from me. 'Oh, hi, Olivia,' I heard her say. 'Shopping? Yes, that sounds great. Sorry? In Paris? Well, I'd love to, but we have to perform every evening. Maybe some other time.' We were little more than five impressionable Irish girls from a Dublin council estate. A day's shopping in Paris was a bit out of our league.

On another occasion, we broke from rehearsals for that Saturday's TV show and were heading off to get some lunch when Stewart Morris asked if we'd follow him into an empty studio. We had no idea why, but obediently did as we were told. Moments later, Donny Osmond walked in followed by his brothers. We couldn't believe our eyes. It was even more exciting than meeting Cliff because we'd known he was coming to the London Room, but we'd had no inkling we

128

were suddenly going to meet our heroes. They looked just like they did on television, handsome, smiling, friendly. The one who immediately caught my eye was Jay, the drummer, but Linda was mad about Donny; she still is. He and his brothers were every bit as nice as you'd expect, chatting and swapping experiences. Then someone had the bright idea of taking a photograph of all of us together. They were trying to make us laugh for the cameras, but I think we were a little shellshocked. After all those years of admiring them from afar, here we were surrounded by them in the flesh. It was such a thrill. The picture somehow found its way into one of the papers the next day. It was accompanied by the witty headline: 'Who are these guys with our Nolans?'

Appearing each week on Cliff's show may have changed our career, but it was exhausting. We had to be at the rehearsal rooms in North Acton by ten each morning; that was over twenty stops on the tube from Ilford. Then we'd be appearing in the London Room each evening, getting home in the small hours, only to be up again early the next day to rehearse for Saturday's TV show. However, that series did exactly what we'd hoped. It turned us into instantly recognisable national faces.

This meant that it became increasingly difficult for us to go out together, because we'd very quickly get besieged by members of the public — but that was lovely, flattering rather than scary. I also got stopped once on Oxford Street by a couple of American tourists, but not because I was a Nolan. 'Oh my God,' said the woman, 'you're the image of our First Lady.' And it was true: in my twenties, I looked a lot like Jackie Kennedy.

We were invited on to every television variety show you can imagine — from *Morecambe and Wise* to *The Two Ronnies* and any number of summertime specials. On more than one occasion, we were on the BBC and ITV at the same time on the same evening. And yet we hadn't even had a hit record.

Because we were signed by Joe Lewis to Hanover Grand, we didn't get any extra money for our TV appearances; the company did. Dad had always been good with money — after all, he'd worked as a bookkeeper back in Dublin — but he had no relevant experience of managing a top act with a national profile. Given our level of success, we should have been infinitely better off than we were. Without Joe's patronage, we'd never have been on television in the first place — we all appreciated that — but I have no memory of our wages ever increasing despite our soaring popularity. In the end, we had to fight to get out of the contract with Hanover Grand that was set to last for six years.

★ ★ ★

We were unaware of all of this in the early days, of course, just happy to get our weekly allowance which we'd blow on the latest fashions in Carnaby Street, and we couldn't complain about repeated television exposure because it only raised our profile. It was also directly responsible for the greatest break of our career, a turn of events beyond our wildest dreams. Our hysteria when we got the news must have been audible all the way from the London Room where we were rehearsing at the time to Blackpool. Dad was ecstatic, Mum was crying, we were screaming and laughing, and all because of a phone call we took from Stewart one afternoon in 1975.

'You're going to open the show for Sinatra,' he said.

Stunned silence.

'You're going to be the opening act on Frank Sinatra's European tour.'

Slowly, the news sank in. We shared Dad's love of Sinatra and, reared on his music by a man who idolised him, we knew just about

131

every word of every song Sinatra had ever sung.

I never did find out quite how we got chosen, but I think a tape of us singing — either on Cliff's show, or of our London Room act — was sent to Sinatra's management. A lot of other tapes were submitted from other groups but, apparently, Sinatra personally picked us. It seemed unbelievable then and, if I'm honest, it still seems unbelievable now. The publicity we received at the time was fantastic. Relatively speaking, only a few thousand people saw us perform with Sinatra — as opposed to the millions who watched us on Cliff's show — but there wasn't a newspaper in the land or a TV news programme that didn't carry the story of five Irish girls landing the gig of a lifetime.

It was to be a two-week tour of the capital cities of Europe, first stop Paris. By then, we'd been totally captivated by the great man. The first time we met him was in rehearsal at the Albert Hall before we embarked on the tour, and we were quickly put at our ease by Frank watching us work and offering helpful tips and encouragement. To be complimented by an artist of his stature was praise indeed. He was convinced, he said, that we'd knock them dead. He was doing his sound checks as were we. He wandered over to us and said, 'You girls won't know any of these songs.' If we'd been less in awe of him we'd have told him that not only did we know those songs but also every other song he'd ever recorded.

He was always relaxed and charming with us. He didn't need to act Mr Big, he was Mr Big. He had nothing to prove. He looked good for a man of sixty. He'd had a hair transplant by then, so he wasn't wearing one of those unconvincing wigs, and he'd put on a little weight to his advantage. It meant he no longer looked rather scrawny. His voice, of course, was extraordinary, every bit as rich and unforced as it was on his records.

At one point, we brought Dad over and asked Sinatra if he'd say hello to one of his biggest fans ever. They shook hands. 'Hello, Tommy,' he said, and then signed a photograph of himself and gave it to my father. I thought Dad was going to faint from pure happiness. I honestly think it was one of the highlights of his life, and we all took genuine pleasure from his pleasure, me included. Years later, he was in mourning for three days when Sinatra died. He just sat at home playing his records. This man had been his idol ever since childhood.

On the opening night in Paris at the Palais des Congrès, Frank invited us down to his dressing room, put his arms around us and said, in a mock Irish accent, 'Come on now, me little girls.' Then someone took a photograph. We've still got it. In the event, that first performance was far from being our best. Bernie had caught a heavy cold so that, when it came to our a cappella version of 'Scarlet Ribbons', she started coughing and couldn't stop. We all felt so sorry for her. I don't think she's got over the embarrassment to this day.

Our act probably lasted about twenty minutes. We opened with our version of The Four Tops' 'Reach Out' and then went into a Judy Garland medley followed by 'Scarlet Ribbons' and then The Osmonds' version of 'I Believe'. Considering nobody knew who we were on the European dates and were only there to see the great man, we went down really well. After our slightly stuttering start in Paris, the rest of the tour was an unforgettable experience and a great success. We went to Brussels, Vienna, Frankfurt and Munich — not that we saw anything other than our hotel rooms and the concert halls where we were performing — before ending up in London. We were meant to do a concert in Berlin, but it was cancelled when the authorities wouldn't guarantee Sinatra's safety while he was in the city.

Frank made sure that, wherever we travelled, we had a limousine of our own, that we didn't travel on the coach with the band. When we'd finished our set each night, he'd allow us to sit on the steps leading down to where he performed in the round. That was a great privilege and a great pleasure, too. Night after night, we'd have the best seats in the house as he sang his way through standard after standard, occasionally looking across to us, smiling and winking. I kept telling myself, Frank Sinatra knows who we are! I kept thinking that, if I pinched myself, I'd wake to discover the whole thing had been a dream.

Finally, we ended up with two nights at the Albert Hall so I got to sing there eventually, which more than made up for the disappointment of Denise and me being thrown off the school coach all those years earlier. It was nerve-racking, but an amazing experience. Mum and Dad came to both London concerts, although they didn't accompany us on the European leg of the tour.

When it was all finally over, Sinatra presented each of us with an engraved gold medallion which he'd had inscribed with the words, 'Love and Peace, Frank Sinatra'. In return, we showed our thanks by buying him a doll for his granddaughter. It's a sign of the man's generosity that, at the after-show party, he left Elizabeth Taylor's side, brushed past a large group of reporters and photographers, and came across to thank us personally for our gift. I speak for all my sisters when I say that we'll never forget the man or his kindness.

As I look back over our entire career — and we had some fabulous experiences — I think that nothing ever eclipsed the Sinatra tour. It was the high spot, no question. We had our own rhythm section — piano, bass, drums, guitar — but all the strings and the brass for our act were provided by Sinatra's sixty-strong orchestra. You might have thought that returning to the nightly demands of the London Room would seem a bit of a comedown after all that we'd experienced on the road with Sinatra, but I think we remained as high as kites for weeks afterwards.

★   ★   ★

As it happens, I have another, quite different reason to remember the Sinatra tour, apart from the thrill of appearing on the same bill as one of the all-time greats. Gene Cherico was the bass player in his backing band and I fancied him almost from the moment we

136

started rehearsing. He was around forty, and not particularly tall: about five foot eight, a couple of inches taller than me. He had dark hair and dark brown eyes behind granny glasses like John Lennon's. He was of medium build and was always smartly dressed onstage and off. If he went outside, he'd put on his Burberry raincoat. He had a lovely smile. I hardly spoke to him all the way through the tour as we criss-crossed Europe but, when we arrived in London, he invited me to a posh restaurant in Park Lane — he was staying at the Hilton — after the second of the two shows at the Royal Albert Hall.

The meal was lovely and he invited me up to his hotel room when we left the restaurant. I didn't need my arm twisting; I was happy to be with him. When we got to his suite, we were kissing and cuddling and then I took my clothes off and climbed into bed. Gene did the same. I'd kissed men before. There was the sailor I'd met on the cruise and there'd been a boy in Blackpool called Pete who would sometimes come with me if I went out dancing, not that my father ever knew about him. But, as soon as Gene put his arm around me, I burst into uncontrollable tears. Sobbing my heart out, I hurriedly dressed and ran out of the hotel. For some reason, I felt guilty and confused and I knew my father wouldn't approve. Before I left, Gene tried to calm me down. He was absolutely lovely, gentle and understanding and reassuring all at once. He must have thought it odd, though, that I was carrying on like this.

I know he really liked me a lot and I liked him, too. He didn't have a wife or girlfriend and I was single. I was twenty-four by then but, when it came to it, the idea of sex, much as I was attracted to him, was too frightening. Half my life away, my father had done something so unforgivable that this was the legacy. Those had been my only sexual experiences. Despite that, my dad had always drummed into me that sex was wrong, sinful, dirty.

It strikes me now as both sad and wicked that two adults who'd formed a bond with each other couldn't go to bed together because my father had made the prospect of intercourse something degrading. I'd never been allowed to feel natural with anyone of the opposite sex. My dad had stunted me emotionally by what he'd done. Somehow, I felt like a child all over again. If I'd been able to analyse my feelings rationally, I think I'd have hated him then as much as I'd done at any point in my life.

Gene wrote to me when he got back to the States, a really sensitive letter, but he must have thought I was nuts. I was a woman behaving like a little girl and not really understanding why. I'd got into that bed of my own accord. It's not as though he'd coerced me. What on earth was the problem? I couldn't have told him, even if I'd wanted to. It's probably why I never replied to his letter. What could I have said? Certainly not the truth, even if I'd sorted out in my head that that was the reason why my nerve had failed.

Every time I looked at my father, a part of me would recall what he'd done to me. I couldn't ever see him simply as my father. I'd look at him and see a dirty old man. Try as I might, it was impossible to expunge those memories, and that's a dreadful legacy with which to be saddled as a grown woman.

7

Losing It

I was twenty-five when I first had sex, with a man I'd met in the Valbonne and who I'd invited to come and visit me one afternoon in the London Room. I'd kissed other men, but never indulged in anything else, not even heavy petting. It wasn't too surprising. My father had made it as difficult as possible for me, and for Denise and Maureen, to have anything to do with boys. He had much less influence over my three youngest sisters because, by the time they were interested in boys, they were much more independent than I'd been.

Any attention that had been paid by boys to the oldest three of us when we performed or toured was swiftly discouraged by him. Any interest one of us might have shown in a particular boy was met with sarcasm and verbal abuse. I clearly remember catching the eye of a boy in a club in Wales. We came off stage and I could tell my father was seething. In front of everyone, he rounded on me.

'I see you're happy to behave like a little

140

slut,' he said, without raising his voice. 'I didn't realise I had a slag for a daughter.'

I was a young woman who'd smiled at a young man she liked the look of. My father's reaction was ridiculously out of proportion, the foul thoughts of a twisted man. He had a very disturbed attitude when it came to sex. There was his private behaviour with me when I was still a child, but now his cruel public comments made me feel that what men wanted was something a young woman should have nothing to do with. The hypocrisy of it all still takes my breath away.

To be honest, I was scared by the whole idea of sex. Kissing boys was nice, but I never wanted to do anything more than that. Deep in my mind lurked the memories of what had happened as I sat on my father's lap when I was twelve, but along with them I had his words ringing in my ears: girls shouldn't have sex before marriage, he'd repeat, over and over again, you might get pregnant which would be a terrible thing. You should only have sex once you're married to the man you love. Sex, he implied, was something dirty and, in my experience, in his hands, he was dead right.

Either way, he'd instilled the fear of God in me. With hindsight, I question his motivation in extolling the virtues of virginity in young women. Part of me believes that he was trying to keep me pure and unsullied, for him. Put simply, I don't think he liked the thought of me being with another man, any other man. Certainly, I know that when I met the man who was to become my husband, my father was jealous of him. He'd bad-mouth him behind my back (I was later told) for no better reason than he was a male competing for my affections.

Of course, saving yourself for the right man, if a little old-fashioned, wasn't necessarily a bad piece of advice, had it come from anyone except my father — but here was a man who'd impregnated his own girlfriend before they'd become man and wife and who'd repeatedly sexually abused his young daughter.

As it transpired, my first sexual encounter at the grand old age of twenty-five, on the dressing-room floor of the London Room in Drury Lane, was far from a pleasurable experience. I was frightened. It hurt. This particular chap had been flirting with me, telling me he loved me even though he had a girlfriend. I was keen on him and I didn't want to become the world's oldest virgin. My experience with Gene was at the back of my mind but, while I was still anxious, I felt it was time to face down my demons. I can't say

142

I enjoyed it, although it did prove one thing: my father had never had full sex with me. That may sound like a strange thing to say, but when you're an innocent who's been abused, it messes with your mind. I didn't know about sex when my father started his campaign of molestation, so I couldn't be sure exactly what he'd done to me. I was pretty certain penetration had never taken place, but then maybe he'd done something to me when I was asleep. All doubts were removed, however, the first time I had full intercourse because I bled. I must have been a virgin.

I went to the man's house a few days later and stayed the night. We had sex again, although I wouldn't take off all my clothes, and it was the first time I'd ever slept in the same bed as someone of the opposite sex. The next morning, however, I heard him on the phone, talking to this other woman and saying the same things to her he'd said to me. So that was the end of that.

★   ★   ★

Luckily, there was the Nolan Sisters' burgeoning career to take my mind off my private life. After our weekly spot on Cliff's Saturday night TV show and then the

143

unforgettable experience of touring with Sinatra, we landed our first summer season the following year, 1976, in Eastbourne. Ronnie Corbett — such a nice man — was the star of the show and impressionist Janet Brown was also on the bill. We barely stopped laughing all summer and it was so different from the sorts of season you get now. There was real money up on that stage. For our act, we had our own scenery and we were also involved in a routine set in a gambling den with dancers dressed as jockeys. It was all very sumptuous, no expense spared.

Our dressing rooms overlooked the tennis courts. I've always been mad about tennis, so I could sit and watch all the top stars playing in the tournament there in the run-up to Wimbledon. I had a grandstand view. It was during our season in Eastbourne that Maureen met John Lloyd, a top British player at the time, so good-looking, and they started going out together. We used to be flown by helicopter to do our show on a Sunday at the London Room by special request from a group of Americans who'd booked the place out and had specified they wanted us to do the cabaret. It was very flattering and exciting, too. We all felt as if we were living a glamorous life in the fast lane.

It was also the same year that we toured

South Africa with Rolf Harris. The scenery was breathtaking, but the temperature was going through the roof. To cool down, we'd take dips in the hotel pool and sip long iced drinks. We'd also visit the sauna as part of our beauty routine. On one visit, we bumped into the almost nude figure of another hotel guest, Tom Jones. He was tall, tanned, with a great physique, just like he looked on TV — and very sexy, a really manly man. We sat and talked music like true professionals before Tom stood up to leave, his towel accidentally falling to the floor as he did so. Stupidly, we all averted our eyes.

Hanover Grand would also loan us out for corporate gigs. I remember once going to Italy to entertain the delegates after some conference or other. It was the first time I'd ever been to Rome. Tommy Cooper was the star turn. We went on first, did a forty-minute act and went off again to warm applause, but as we exited into the wings there, lying on a stretcher backstage, was Tommy; he'd had a heart attack. It was such a shock. He was breathing but he was deathly white. The organisers told us to turn around and go straight back onstage. We hadn't really rehearsed any more numbers, but luckily we were being backed by our own band, so we'd call out the title of a song and off they'd go.

In the end, we did another half hour as poor Tommy was rushed to hospital. He pulled through, but as all the world knows, it was a heart attack on live TV that killed him eight years later.

Life-changing events seem to happen to me at Christmas and 1976 was no exception. That was the day I first set eyes on Brian Wilson, a professional football player with Blackpool and the possessor of the most indelible blue eyes I'd ever seen. He was sitting among a group of footballers in the Bloomfield Working Men's Club near Blackpool FC's ground where my brother Tommy was the resident drummer. My younger brother Brian was a good friend of this other Brian, as it turned out.

We were briefly introduced and the second thing that struck me about him was his Geordie accent; he seemed like a character straight out of a Catherine Cookson story. He was nineteen although he seemed much older because he'd been signed to the club, I later discovered, at fifteen and had lived away from home since then. I was twenty-six but, despite my show business experience, still rather immature and naïve for my age.

There was a party at my Aunt Teresa's house on Boxing Day evening. Brian was playing football in the afternoon and then he came to join us when the match was over. To my disappointment he spent the whole night talking to Linda Gallagher, who was back in Blackpool for the Christmas break, but by the end of the party we'd managed to have a short chat and he asked me if I wanted to go out for a drink with him the following day.

We got on from the start. He was quiet and thoughtful; he had a gentle nature, and talked a lot about his upbringing and his family in Newcastle. He used to say that, later on in his life, he'd like to be a lumberjack in the wilds of Canada. He was attracted by the simple life. He also dreamed of taking off round the world in one of those big camper vans. He never shirked his responsibilities, but I think a part of him yearned for the open road. He was one of those people everybody liked; he was a good listener and always willing to help anyone in a spot of bother.

He was fond of playing the guitar, just sitting in the corner at a party on his own. He couldn't sing, but he'd pick out the tune for John Denver's big hit, 'Annie's Song', and I'd sing while he played. If I had a day off, I'd go back to Blackpool to see him. We'd meet and I'd always fall into a pattern of teasing him. I don't know why; maybe because it was all so pressured, having to meet so infrequently, and this was a sort of nervous reaction. In

147

time, he'd walk me back to where he lived. We'd pass someone's garden and he might pick a rose and present it to me.

Brian was quite tall — just under six feet — and broad-shouldered, lean rather than thin, and strong. His legs were muscular, as you'd expect with a super-fit professional football player. When we first met, he had blondish, slightly mousey hair which he wore to just below his ears. He'd only wear smart clothes for a special occasion, but he looked great in a suit because he had such a good physique. Being sporty, though, he tended to go for leisurewear the rest of the time: tracksuit bottoms or jeans with a T-shirt. In the summer, it was always shorts. On his feet, he liked to wear trainers or moccasin-type slippers; I remember on one occasion that he came to meet me off the train in those slippers. People were pointing at him, but he didn't care.

He was always scrupulously clean. He'd shower and wash his hair twice a day because he'd be training a lot. He had nice hands and his nails were always clipped and clean. One of the things I liked best about him was his arms. They were toned rather than too muscular — I don't like muscle men — but they were strong. When he put those arms around me, I felt safe and protected. Even after he gave up football, he still continued to train two or three times a week and coach amateur teams. He used to run a lot and go to the gym to use the treadmill or the bike or the cross-trainer, so his physique didn't really change.

I know there's six and a half years between us, but you'd never have known then that Brian was younger than me. We looked right together. Ours was turning into a serious relationship and I started staying the night with Brian at his digs if ever I was in Blackpool. I didn't particularly advertise the fact to my father, but I wouldn't have cared if he'd known. I was twenty-six now; I could please myself. I'd had a pretty chequered sex life, to say the very least, and I certainly wasn't relaxed with Brian in the beginning. Understandably, I was apprehensive — I'd never had an open sexual relationship with anybody; I didn't really know what to do; I might just as well have been a virgin — but I knew it would be all right in the end because Brian was so gentle, so considerate, so patient. If I flinched or displayed any hint of anxiety, he'd ask me if I was all right. He was the person who turned sex into making love.

It was an unusual courtship, conducted almost entirely on the phone. With him travelling all over the country with his football team and the increasing popularity of the Nolan Sisters causing us to tour extensively, it was always difficult for us to find time to be together. On one occasion, we arranged to meet in the less-than-romantic setting of a motorway service station, but what was the choice?

Brian was absolutely dedicated to his football. I later learned that scouts for Manchester United, Everton, Liverpool and Nottingham Forest had all wanted to sign him up, but, for some reason, his father had decided that Blackpool would suit him better; it was a smaller club, he was a young lad and he wouldn't be overwhelmed by the experience. Initially, he lived in miserable digs opposite the football ground with no hot water throughout a freezing winter. His mother came up on a visit and insisted on seeing the club's manager. Either he must find somewhere better for her son to live, she said, or she'd be taking him home. He was quickly rehoused. Clearly, he had talent but, unfortunately, at seventeen, he'd suffered a bad injury which resulted in the cartilage being removed from his knee. Then he damaged his ankle. In the end, these injuries meant he had to finish his career before he reached thirty.

Against the odds, given the clashing

demands on our time, we grew closer and closer. We'd always start our daily phone conversations — often three or four every day — by saying how much we were missing each other. We were getting more and more open about our feelings. One day, at the end of the conversation, he suddenly said, 'I love you.' It was the sweetest moment. I immediately repeated the same three words back to him. From that moment on, we never ended a conversation without saying, 'I love you.' We'd also exchange letters in which we said how much we wanted to be together for ever.

As my relationship with Brian deepened and matured so my career with my sisters flourished. We were still appearing regularly at the London Room, but Hanover Grand, who effectively owned us, would release us from our engagement there if something prestigious and lucrative enough was offered. In 1977, just such an offer was forthcoming with the invitation for us to appear in New York at the Westchester Premier Theatre for two weeks as the support act to Engelbert Humperdinck. He was an enormous star in the States at the time, although no one had the first idea who *we* were. It didn't matter. There was a real buzz around him and that rubbed off on us.

It was the first time we'd been to America

and I'll never forget it. We stayed at a five-star hotel, the like of which we'd never seen before. Mum and Dad came with us and it was like the realisation of a family dream. My father may have been fiercely patriotic about Ireland, but he loved the States. As we were growing up, he was forever telling us that it was the best country in the world. And now here we all were. It was a huge thrill — and I didn't mind him being there. I was secure in my relationship with Brian, something my father must have seen for himself, and that gave me real strength.

We didn't get to know Engelbert well. We'd chat to him and he was pleasant, but, unlike Tom Jones who was natural, down-to-earth and hadn't lost his Welsh accent, Engelbert had acquired something of a mid-Atlantic twang to his voice and seemed very caught up in the whole showbiz razzmatazz. You got the impression, without being unkind about it, that he rather believed his own publicity, as they say.

Like Tom, he had a reputation for liking the ladies, but he certainly didn't flirt with any of us. Anyway, he had enough beautiful women throwing themselves at him. There's also another reason why we'd never have crossed his radar in that way. Because we were five sisters — this was before Coleen had joined the group — we were seen as a family act and somehow were never allowed to grow up in people's eyes as individual adult women. I was twenty-seven by then, but still I felt I needed my father's permission to do anything. Having said that, and although she did nothing to encourage it, all the men fell in love with Maureen, no matter where we went. You could see why: she was the prettiest of all of us, a striking brunette with a lovely personality.

In the spring of 1978, fifteen months after we'd first met, Brian and I got engaged. It happened during one of our interminable telephone conversations. In fact, I was the one who asked Brian if he'd like to get engaged and he said yes, he would but, if that were the case, he didn't want a ten-year engagement. 'If we're getting engaged,' he said, 'we're getting married.' My instinctive reaction once we'd finished our conversation was to call my Aunt Teresa. She was thrilled. Then she told me my mum and dad were with her. Did I want to tell them? I told her no, I didn't, but she could. As it was, Aunt Teresa told my parents my news, but they didn't bother to pick up the phone to congratulate me. To tell the truth, I was quite relieved because I was worried about my father's reaction. My childhood experience at his hands had frightened me in all my dealings with him. The abuse may have happened a long time ago, but in my mind it had never gone away. So at what should have been a moment of uncomplicated happiness and joy — telling my parents I was going to marry the love of my life — I shied away, the thought of breaking the news to my own father instantly becoming an obstacle I wanted to avoid. That man cheated me out of so much in my life by what he did to me and I can never forgive him for that.

I don't think I spelled out my feelings to myself quite as clearly as that at the time, but my emotions were wobbly and it wasn't too hard to work out why. It was then that I decided to tell Brian the secret I'd hugged to myself for all those years, but this was something that couldn't be done over the phone.

When Brian made a rare visit to our home in Granville Road, Ilford, just a matter of days later, I knew that the moment had arrived. We were sitting on the stairs leading to the first floor — it is as clear to me now as if it had happened yesterday — and I remember feeling overwhelmed with apprehension about how I was going to broach the subject. In the end, I just blurted it out.

'My dad sexually abused me when I was a child,' I said.

'You're kidding,' he exclaimed. I don't blame him for being so shocked. We sat together quietly, and then, after a long pause, he said, 'What did he do to you?'

I did my best to explain what had happened. I told him it was one-sided, that I was, quite literally, an innocent victim, and it was only as I moved into my teens that I understood how wrong it had been. I explained that my naïvety was overtaken by incredulity and anger as the full impact of how my innocence had been exploited fully hit me. Brian was thoughtful for a very long time.

Then he said, 'So you never had intercourse?' I told him no.

I think he was in shock. He didn't ask me how I felt about what happened because he was obviously finding it hard to absorb what he'd just been told. I could see it was almost too much for him to take in. I didn't blame him. In fact, my overwhelming emotion was one of relief. I was just glad that at last I'd been able to share my secret with the one person I loved and trusted more than any other in my life.

In no way did Brian blame me for what had happened. He saw me, quite properly, as a victim, but I often wonder whether he always thought I should have done something about what was going on, that I should have spoken out at the time. When I eventually made the decision to tell Brian my story, I warned him there was no point saying anything to anybody else because I'd always deny it. I can only think I was still frightened of my father. Why else would I want to protect him? It must also be true that I wanted to protect myself. Nor did Brian try to persuade me to speak out.

A part of me wishes, though, that Brian *had* taken matters into his own hands. He was the man in my life now. He could have confronted my dad, and then maybe I'd have felt strong enough to confirm the whole story. And, even if he didn't say something when I first told him my story, I sometimes wonder if he wanted to speak out when our daughters were born. To this day, I think Brian feels guilty about keeping quiet.

My revelations changed his relationship with my father, of course. He would never have made a scene because he simply wasn't that kind of person, but he became very cold towards him. I can't prove this but I'm sure my dad sensed the difference in Brian's behaviour. Brian was good at putting on a front in his dealings with my father if other people were around, but virtually ignored him if ever he and I were alone with him. When he

156

first knew my father, they might go to the pub together for a drink. Not any more. Brian always found an excuse to get out of it. No one else would ever have known that my father had spotted the subtle change in Brian's attitude towards him. But I could. I'm certain to this day that he'd worked out I'd told Brian about the sexual abuse, not, of course, that I can ever prove this because my dad, as ever, never acknowledged that anything had happened.

If I had thought that Brian would in some way cool towards me as a result of what I'd told him, I needn't have worried. Not long afterwards, he bought me an engagement ring off his own bat, a solitaire diamond. I'd described what I wanted, but a lot of men wouldn't have gone out on their own and chosen it. We were appearing at a club called Talk of the North, between Blackpool and Wigan, and decided to make one evening there our engagement party, so we hired a coach and all our friends came over, watched the show and then celebrated afterwards. John Lloyd was going out with Maureen at the time and I remember him turning up in a white suit. Unfortunately, someone spilled a glass of red wine over him by mistake, but he didn't make any fuss about it at all. He was a very nice man — much too nice for

Maureen, she always said!

Then I discovered I was pregnant.

I missed two periods before I took a pregnancy test which proved positive. We'd used no protection when we'd made love so what did I expect? On the other hand, I'd never seen a condom in my life. Still, Brian might have worked out it would have been a good idea to use one! I knew by then that he was the one for me so at first I wasn't as upset as I might have been, but that mood quickly passed. There were other things to consider.

I may have been nearly twenty-eight, but the shame it would have brought on my family, and on the image of the squeaky-clean Nolan Sisters, was something I couldn't contemplate. Also, although we were engaged, Brian and I weren't ready to start a family. However, easily the most terrifying thought of all was the prospect of telling my father. I shook with fear when I thought of his reaction. I was also concerned about what my mum would think. Brian and I agonised over the best course of action, but we could see no other alternative: I decided an abortion was my only option. We phoned a clinic in Manchester to find out all the details involved and how much it would cost.

Then fate took a hand. We were appearing

at the ABC Theatre, Blackpool, with The Bachelors topping the bill, and I must have been about three months into the pregnancy. I was in a restaurant with Brian one evening when I was suddenly gripped by the most excruciating pain in my abdomen. I was so naïve, it never occurred to me that I might be losing the baby. We were staying at my Aunt Teresa's at the time, while she was away on holiday, so that we could be together. The pain subsided, but later, in the middle of the night, I woke up and I was bleeding. I assured Brian that it wasn't too bad and that we ought to wait until the morning to see what to do next.

The following day, I was on stage performing a song called 'Be A Clown'. We were all dressed in appropriate costumes as we leap-frogged over each other's backs. The pain started again and this time it was really unbearable. I just about made it to the interval and then went back to our dressing room where I slid down the wall in agony.

'What's wrong, Anne?' Maureen said, her face etched with anxiety.

'I think I'm having a miscarriage,' I replied, between agonised gasps.

There was a stunned silence. Brian had been the only other living soul who'd known I was pregnant. Maureen was the first to come to her senses. 'We'd better get you to the hospital,' she exclaimed.

'Don't worry,' I said, with more conviction than I felt, 'I'll be all right.'

But I wasn't. My sisters phoned Brian and he rushed to be there with me. I miscarried that same evening. The decision about what to do with the pregnancy had been taken out of my hands. I was raised a Catholic and I believe to this day that I couldn't have coped with my conscience had I gone through with the termination.

Mum and Dad had to be told I was in hospital, of course, and naturally the first thing they wanted to know was what was wrong with me. To my surprise, instead of judging me they were both more concerned that I was going to make a full recovery, their relief overcoming any embarrassment or, in the case of my father, any show of anger.

For once in his life, my dad had put me first.

8

Hits and Highlights

Between 1974 and 1978 — the year before Brian and I got married — the Nolan Sisters recorded eight singles for Target Records, a subsidiary of Warner Brothers. All of them failed to make the charts. Looking back now, it's not hard to see why. Our image was designed to appeal to an older generation, not the predominantly young record-buying public. We also recorded a limited edition album for London Room audiences which sold well in the club at the end of each show, but was never destined to make the national Top Twenty.

Throughout our whole career, it was working in a recording studio I liked the least. Live performances were exciting, with all that adrenaline pumping round your body; and I always enjoyed appearing on television, whether singing or being interviewed. When we were recording a new single or tracks for an album, however, Bernie would usually be singing the lead while the rest of us were doing the doo-wops in the background, and when you had to repeat the same line over and over again, it became just demanding and boring. It would have been quite different, of course, had I been a solo artist, but the most I could expect was to take the lead on one song on an album.

★   ★   ★

'Girls, you're going to Liverpool,' announced Joe Lewis one day. 'I've made arrangements for you to appear twice — lunchtime and evening — at a beautiful club up there. The audiences are wonderful. You'll have a lovely time.' This was to be a one-off engagement only.

We didn't doubt it. Having lived for so long in nearby Blackpool, we'd played more Merseyside clubs than we could count and we'd always been struck by the warmth of the reception. We looked forward to the gig. Playing the London Room was a great experience, but, as any performer will testify, a residency can take the edge off your performance. To have the chance to play another venue was always welcome.

The first thing we noticed as we took to the stage was that there were no women in the audience. The club was buzzing with the conversation of men sitting around, smoking and drinking. 'Something's wrong,' I whispered out of the corner of my mouth to my nearest sister. She gave a slightly nervous smile and nodded her agreement.

Lined up in our virginal white suits, we swung into our sweet Judy Garland medley, all the time puzzling about the crowd in front of us. We could hear tittering from different sections of the audience but, seasoned professionals that we were, we soldiered on. Our harmonies filled the room. The reaction, polite at first, gradually grew in strength and volume. By the end of the set, we'd won them over and walked off to rapturous applause with shouts of 'More!' ringing in our ears. It was only then we found out that, while the male audience had clearly enjoyed our performance, they were more used to ogling female strippers over their Sunday lunchtime drinks.

★   ★   ★

In 1977, WEA, our record label's mother company, came up with the idea of picking twenty of the most popular songs of the day and then canvassing opinion throughout the UK to choose who would record them. Our TV appearances had lodged us firmly in the popular imagination and, to our surprise and delight, we topped the poll. In February the following year, *20 Giant Hits* was released and quickly rose to the top of the charts. At last we had our first gold disc and the bona fide recording success we'd craved for so long.

That's when we left Hanover Grand. I didn't know the details at the time because our father did the deal. It was only later I discovered that it had cost us an enormous amount of money to terminate our contract, a move that, while winning us our freedom, almost put us back on the bread-line. I never did find out how much we had to pay, but, considering that we received not one penny's profit from the £300,000 generated by sales of the album — that all went, perfectly legitimately, to Hanover Grand — I can only think it must have been a very substantial sum.

Any misgivings over this move were soon dispelled when Dad explained that WEA were offering us a long-term recording contract and CBS were also making their interest known. My father was still advising us, but, although we'd listen to him, ultimately we made our own decisions. He was no longer singing at the London Room. He'd left shortly before us and, although we still all lived in Granville Road together, his influence on us was receding. We were so busy, we saw very little of him, but, if I ever found myself alone with him, I'd still leave the room, even though I'd have been able to deal with any nonsense if he'd ever tried anything. My relationship with Brian had altered my life. I now felt confident and able to look after myself.

In the end, it was CBS who signed us but insisted we change our name to, simply, the Nolans. I think they felt it was a bit snappier, a bit less old-fashioned than the Nolan Sisters. We were euphoric. Then came a bombshell: Denise wanted to quit the group and go solo. She'd always hated having to learn choreographed dance routines; I think she also relished the opportunity of tackling big, dramatic numbers on her own. We understood her reasons for going but it made us apprehensive as she was a very popular member of the line-up. In the event, we regrouped and felt we were still capable of making more or less the same sound. The brand that was the Nolans was bigger, it seemed, than any individual member.

As it turned out, Denise got lots of work and, although she never had solo recording success, she was happy. We loved her, we missed her, but we respected her decision. Being sisters always came before the music,

165

but we were still individuals. Denise was the first to follow her dream and, even though it was painful, no one tried to stand in her way.

The second setback of that year was losing out on our chance to represent Britain in the *Eurovision Song Contest*. Many people poke fun at *Eurovision* for being too cheesy, but that was a charge also continually levelled at us, something we'd long stopped minding about, and we knew how important it was to have the chance of exposure to a television audience in excess of 500 million people. Appearing on *Eurovision* would really put us on the map.

We'd been rehearsing a song called 'Harry, My Honolulu Lover' for weeks before the ultimate UK *Eurovision* entry was to be chosen by a panel of judges. Our appearance would be of vital importance, and we looked great (or so we were told) in Hawaiian-style mini-skirts and garlands of flowers round our necks. We had a tightly choreographed dance routine, and felt our chances of being chosen were good, but all hopes were dashed when a strike by BBC technicians made it impossible for us to perform live. With only the record for the panel to listen to, and no visual presentation, we were denied our chance to shine, ending up fourth.

There was a big compensation round the

166

corner, though. We were invited to appear on the *Royal Variety Show* in November 1978 at the London Palladium in the presence of the Queen Mother, with Gracie Fields topping the bill. We had just the one song on that occasion — 'I've Got My Love To Keep Me Warm' — but Alyn Ainsworth had arranged five-part harmonies and there were intricate dance steps to remember. It was a dream come true; five years earlier, we'd been singing in Blackpool clubs. We were dying with nerves before we went on so the choreographer gave us each a glass of wine, which didn't make any difference at all. I needed the whole bottle just to myself!

While there were peaks and troughs on the professional front, in my private life I could not have been more happy. Brian and I set a date in June 1979 for our wedding at the Sacred Heart Church in Talbot Square, Blackpool. My sisters were thrilled for my personal happiness but a little apprehensive, I think, about the potential impact of my marriage on the act. They did nothing to try to dissuade me from marrying Brian, of course, and they were almost as excited as me about the June wedding. But, equally, it must have been pretty clear that the prospect of my marriage was more important to me than a singing career — and supposing I wanted a

167

family? Might I also be on the point of leaving the act?

They were quite right to be worried, of course, although Coleen was waiting in the wings. She was then fourteen. Give her a few more months to learn all the words and dance routines, they said, and then I'd be free to make any decision I wanted. I agreed. What were a few more months? Brian and I had our whole lives together. Or so I thought.

As it turned out, it was a wonder I got married at all. The big day dawned. My wedding dress had been made specially for me by Jo Quill, who'd designed our stage wear. It was her wedding gift to me and I couldn't have been happier with it. The problem on the day itself, however, was one of logistics: my hairdresser, Delma, agreed to do my hair, but it would be easier, she said, if I came to her house.

'Are you nervous?' she asked when I arrived. I said I wasn't, but she ignored me and handed me what she described as 'a little drink', which turned out to be more like a treble Martini. We were nattering away and I was becoming more and more relaxed, a warm, mellow feeling spreading through my body as she titivated my coiffure. It was only when Delma was applying the finishing touches that she casually asked the time of the service.

'Two o'clock,' I said.

She squealed. 'Well, it's already half past one!'

How I made it from her house to my parents', threw on my bridal gown and got into the landau to travel — at snail's pace — to the church before everyone packed up and went home, I'll never know. I didn't have time to put on any make-up but luckily we'd been working on a Caribbean cruise just two weeks earlier, so I was nice and brown. In the end, I was only twenty minutes late.

Delma's shot of alcohol had steadied me but, nonetheless, I felt a bit strange on the way to the church. Even on my wedding day, when I should have been holding Dad's hand and thanking him for everything he'd done for me, I was conscious of sitting as far apart from him as possible. Fortunately, we were in an open carriage with people lining the streets and waving, so I concentrated on smiling and waving back. I'd have found it much more difficult if we'd been together in a car, in an enclosed space, and having to chat to him. As it was, I don't think we exchanged more than two words. What a relief — and what a sad thing to have to say about your own father on your wedding day.

As we approached Talbot Square, I'd never seen a crowd like it. The whole square had been closed to traffic, there were mounted police everywhere, my ears were ringing with the cheers and applause from fans of the Nolans — and yet being so near to my father meant I couldn't fully savour the magic of this unfolding spectacle. We finally reached the church and I was helped down from the landau. Then I had to link arms with him as we made our way through the scrum of photographers — the papers were full of pictures the next day — to get into the church and begin the walk down the aisle, an iconic moment in any woman's life but tainted for me for reasons only two other people in the world knew about: my father and my husband-to-be.

For all that, my overwhelming feeling was one of happiness. This was the best day of my life and a brand new start with the man I loved and trusted. When the priest reached the part in the ceremony when he asked: 'Who gives this woman to be married?' and my dad said, 'I do,' I thought, 'That's it. I'm free. Now I can get on with the rest of my life.'

My sisters, in true family tradition, had decided to sing a beautiful, intricate, unaccompanied version of The Carpenters'

'We've Only Just Begun', scored by the BBC's Johnny Coleman. The only problem was that the various demands on their time meant they'd barely rehearsed it. To this day, I maintain I heard nothing wrong with their interpretation of the song, but Maureen — she always sang the lower harmony — complained that her part was so down in her boots, she sounded as if she was farting!

Linda, standing just behind her, apparently started shaking with laughter (she always shakes when she laughs), followed closely by Denise and Coleen. Bernie alone is blessed with the ability to control her mirth and managed to keep a straight face. Luckily, none of them was in my line of vision, otherwise I'd probably have been infected by the giggles as well. In the event, and in true professional fashion, they finished the song and I thought it was beautiful.

As the evening wore on at the reception at the St Ives Hotel, guests began asking if I'd sing a song. In the end, I agreed and gave my rendition of 'Why Did I Choose You?' which contains the line, 'If I had to choose again, I would still choose you.' As I finished, I looked across at my beloved, my brand new husband — at that moment sprawled across the floor, his back against the stage, in total oblivion and feeling no pain. Brian liked his

171

drink; he was no different from any other young footballer: a few drinks after the match and maybe the next day, too, and then he'd be back in training for the following Saturday's game. He'd booked the honeymoon suite at a local hotel, the Norbreck Castle, and he'd sobered up by then so, yes, it was a lovely night! The next day we went off on our honeymoon to the holy island of Lindisfarne, near Newcastle. We stayed for two weeks in a lovely cottage lent to us by a friend and the weather was terrible. I couldn't have cared less. It had been Brian's choice and a surprise for me. The peace and quiet were a wonderful respite from the hectic existence each of us had been used to. There were only two pubs on the island and Brian said I managed to drink them both dry of wine, so that they had to send to the mainland for more!

He was so loving, so thoughtful, so supportive. He always called me his pet lamb. Whenever we went out for a drink together — this started long before we got married — he'd split open one of the beer mats and write me little poems and love messages on them. I saved them all and then, on our first wedding anniversary, I paid someone to print them all in a book with Brian's initials on the cover.

We'd bought a small, modern semi-detached house in Harcourt Road in Blackpool. It was the first place we'd owned and could call ours, the first place where Brian and I could be alone together. I loved it. There was a tiny kitchen/diner on the left off the hallway and the lounge to the right with French windows leading on to the small garden. There were three bedrooms upstairs and a bathroom and toilet. However, we'd barely returned there from our honeymoon before Brian was back playing football and I was booked with my sisters for a headlining three-month summer season at Cleethorpes on the Lincolnshire coast.

I hardly saw anything of my new husband and I really minded. I longed to be with Brian, even though there were fun times to be had during those three months. On one occasion, the stage crew replaced our microphones with ice-cream cones, so that we swept on stage, reached out for our mikes and then discovered the awful truth. The only answer was to lick them as if this was part of the act, something that cracked up the audience and put them in the best of moods as the real microphones were then placed in our hands.

Sometimes, the mistakes were genuine. I remember when we were playing the Talk of the North in Charnock Richard there were several quick changes necessary, and we had to rush from the stage to our dressing room in the breaks between numbers to clamber quickly into matching outfits. On this particular night, we all arrived back on stage, slightly out of breath, me in a dress about four inches too short and baggy round the bosom and Linda (shorter than me but more generously endowed) with her hem round her ankles and busting out all over in the boob department.

That was the year, too, of our first *Top of the Pops* appearance. It was a big deal for us because here was a programme we'd all watched as we'd been growing up, but we'd never dared hope that one day we might actually perform on it. It was great: we could wear the type of clothes that girls of our age wore in real life, not the ageing costumes designed for us by wardrobe departments. If I see pictures of us now in our Spandex trousers, I cringe. They were very fashionable at the end of the seventies, but even so, surrounded by all those punk bands, we were like fish out of water. We didn't care. We had a great time.

Our eventual arrival on the national scene and particularly in the pop charts occurred well after the heyday of both The Beatles and

174

The Stones. As luck would have it, the greatest success of the butter-wouldn't-melt-in-your-mouth Nolans coincided with the arrival of punk rock, and we'd be on *Top of the Pops* alongside the Sex Pistols, which must have seemed very incongruous at the time; one of them even spat on our dressing-room door, presumably because that's what he thought a punk ought to do. Bless!

Years later, we got a letter from Kevin Rowland, lead singer with Dexy's Midnight Runners. He was going through an intense counselling course at the time — for whatever reason — and he wrote to apologise for saying nasty things about us. This came as something of a surprise, since none of us could remember his ever saying anything unpleasant to our faces, but part of the recovery programme, apparently, was that you said sorry to anyone you'd insulted when you were in the grip of your demons.

On *Top of the Pops* each week, there was a live orchestra employed by the BBC. None of the punk groups performed live versions of their hits; they'd simply mime to whatever their record in the charts was at the time. However, we were long used to singing live so were asked to appear almost every week, and that justified the booking of the orchestra. It

175

was rather unfair on us because the version we did in the TV studio, while musically note perfect, never sounded like the recorded version, whereas, when it came to the punks, the TV audience at home heard their records in exactly the same way as they did on the radio.

For our first performance on *Top of the Pops*, we sang 'Spirit, Body and Soul' written by Bruce Welch and Hank Marvin of The Shadows. Bruce, a really nice, down-to-earth chap and extremely talented, produced a lot of our records. That single managed to get into the lower reaches of the charts, our first, modest success. Never mind: a bigger one was just round the corner.

When I first heard 'I'm In The Mood For Dancing' written by Ben Findon and Mike Myers, I didn't like it at all, but then I was always hopeless at spotting a potential hit. On this occasion, though, none of my sisters liked it either. What did we know? It turned out to be the biggest single success of our entire career, spending sixteen weeks in the UK Top 20, three of them at Number 3 in the charts; it was also a hit all over Europe, and was Number One in Japan where our popularity not only rivalled that of The Beatles, it surpassed it! We were in demand as never before, touring the UK, Europe and our native Ireland. We also received an invitation to appear at the prestigious Montreux Song Festival where we met the distinguished violinist Stéfane Grappelli. At last the Nolans were enjoying the sort of success about which we'd always dreamed.

I still think 'I'm In the Mood For Dancing' sounds good today, but we didn't half get sick of singing it in 1980. We were invited on to every TV and radio show imaginable and there was only one song everyone wanted to hear. It's still played to this day. My daughters go out to discos and they come home and tell me they've been dancing to their mother's record. Even now I get cheques every so often for however many times it's been played on the radio, a hundred pounds or so once in a while and always very welcome, not least because it's unexpected.

It was an extraordinarily exciting time. After learning our craft with all those years spent on the working men's club circuit, we were now major stars, the most successful female band in Britain. Everything we did, it seemed, turned to gold. We were on a roll and it was difficult not to feel heady most of the time.

By now, we girls were travelling by luxurious coach complete with beds and TVs. We were touring, doing one-nighters in

177

different towns and commanding as much as £10,000 for a single gig. That had to be split six ways, of course — my dad still took his cut — and you'd have to put a proportion of your earnings aside for tax, as well as making your contribution to the five crew members and five band members who travelled everywhere with us, so really our wages never properly reflected our success.

It was in 1980 that we landed a sixteen-week summer season at the Blackpool Opera House, with Mike Yarwood topping the bill. They always say that he was something of a tortured genius, but I never detected any of that. He was easy and relaxed in our company, with no airs and graces, but then I always thought he had a bit of a thing for Linda. I think she liked him, too, but he was married and nothing ever happened. He certainly had a twinkle in his eye, though, whenever he talked to her. It was no more than harmless flirting.

The Opera House holds more than 3,500 people and every performance was packed out. Nowadays, it's never full unless someone of the stature of Tom Jones or Shirley Bassey is topping the bill. I can't honestly say I felt nervous about singing in front of so vast a crowd. On the Sinatra tour, we'd sometimes played to houses of 10,000. People who hadn't seen us before assumed we were overnight successes, but we'd done ten years singing in working men's clubs. Don't let the figures fool you. Yes, the clubs might hold on average only about three hundred punters, but they're the most difficult audience in the world to win over. They want to chat and drink their beer. They don't want to be interrupted by a stage act. If they don't like you, they won't listen or, worse still, they walk out. In a theatre, people have paid for their seats; they've come to watch you perform; they start by being on your side. So it wasn't nerve-racking. You could feel the warmth of affection from the auditorium coming over the footlights.

I couldn't have been happier. We were earning good money, we were performing in our home town to appreciative audiences, and it meant, most importantly of all, that Brian and I could be with each other all the time, living in our own house. Life was good.

★　★　★

Nothing lasts for ever, however, and during that summer Brian's relationship with Blackpool FC in general, and its manager in particular, came to a head. He was put on the transfer list and was eventually sold to

179

Torquay United. We didn't want to be apart, but there didn't seem much choice. So, in the September, Brian moved down to Devon and I carried on until the summer season ended the following month.

I longed to join him, and even more so now because I was pregnant. The show hadn't been running long when I'd started to feel unwell. It wasn't too difficult to diagnose the cause, a suspicion confirmed by a home pregnancy kit. This time I was married and I couldn't have been happier, even though I suffered from blinding headaches and sickness throughout the full nine months. I also developed an aversion to tea; I couldn't stand the smell of it. I didn't care. This was the realisation of a long-held dream.

The end of the season and my future commitments left me little choice but to tell my sisters I'd be leaving the group. To be honest, I'd been wanting to for some time, for the simple reason that I wanted to be with Brian. They understood completely, and I thought I'd be heading south without so much as a glance over my shoulder, but for nineteen years I'd rehearsed, performed, toured, eaten, slept, drunk and lived the life of my siblings, and now, almost suddenly, it was coming to an end. I felt such a mix of emotions. I longed to be a full-time wife and mother but, equally, I knew I'd miss singing with my sisters.

One of the best songs in our repertoire was an a cappella version of Cliff Richard's 'Miss You Nights'. The last time we sang it, during our final performance at the Opera House, I couldn't finish. I broke down in tears as young Coleen walked from the wings and took over my part. By the time she'd finished, there wasn't a dry eye in the house. It was the end of an era. Maureen, Linda, Bernie and Coleen then headed off to Japan where 'I'm In The Mood for Dancing' had become the first record ever to top the Japanese domestic and international charts at the same time.

Meanwhile, I headed off to Torquay — and a close brush with death.

9

Amy Makes Three

We'd sold our little house in Blackpool and eventually bought a semi in Roselands Drive, Paignton, a small town just along the coast from Torquay. It was a lovely spot and our back garden overlooked the bay. However, when I first arrived in Devon in the November, nearly six months pregnant, Brian and I shared a house with another footballer, Tommy Sermanni, who'd played alongside him in Blackpool and also been transferred to Torquay, although a month earlier. This was a stopgap until we found our own place. Tommy was fabulous: he couldn't have been more welcoming or friendly. Never once did he make us feel we were invading his space or getting in his way.

For years and years, I'd yearned for a normal life. My ambitions may sound modest, but I longed for a husband to love, a baby to cherish and a home of our own. Now it was about to happen. It's impossible to exaggerate my feeling of joy, but don't misunderstand me. I wouldn't have missed the richness of my show business experiences and achievements for the world. No one could take away from me the successes I'd had with my sisters. These were mine to savour for ever. I considered myself privileged. We all felt like that. It almost beggars belief that five girls from a council estate in Dublin should have become major stars in Britain and beyond. We'd shared a stage with incredible entertainers, international icons like Frank Sinatra, Engelbert Humperdinck, Cliff Richard, Morecambe and Wise and Tommy Cooper, but we'd never got too big for our boots. If ever any one of us started putting on airs and graces, the rest of us would be down on her like a ton of bricks.

It had been an incredible life, comfortably exceeding our most far-fetched fantasies, but it had effectively robbed me of my teenage years and dominated most of my twenties. Now, though, I was embarking on a new life, a world away from suitcases and aeroplanes, anonymous hotel rooms and tour buses, cameras and lights and TV studios. To anyone else, what lay ahead might have seemed mundane. To me, it was the beginning of my greatest adventure ever. I was about to have a family of my own. Nothing and no one — not even my father — could taint it or take it away from me.

As anyone who knows it will tell you, Torquay is built on a series of hills. Brian would take the car to work and I'd be climbing up and down those hills on foot, carrying home heavy bags of shopping. It was good exercise but, as my pregnancy progressed, it became too strenuous for my condition. Still, I felt healthy and I was happy, so I carried on regardless. Brian could not have been more attentive. He was as excited as me about the imminent birth of our first child.

Towards the end of my pregnancy, and before my mother came to stay in preparation for the baby's birth, my sisters embarked on a UK tour which brought them to Paignton. Naturally, I was in the audience with Brian, and with Jean Lane, a friend I'd made locally. I can't say I was too surprised when the girls announced to the audience my presence in the theatre, but I admit to feeling a bit self-conscious when they insisted I join them on stage. Maureen, Linda, Bernie and Coleen looked so slim and sleek, kitted out in their beautiful dresses, whereas I felt rather a frump in my maternity smock, but I knew I couldn't refuse. When the applause died down, the girls gathered round me. 'Anne,' said Maureen, 'we have a surprise for you,' and so saying, they presented me with a platinum disc of 'I'm In The Mood For Dancing', awarded for sales in excess of over half a million copies in the UK alone. I shall never forget the feeling of euphoria that swept over me. However, it didn't make me feel I wanted to be back in the group. My ambitions now were firmly rooted in domesticity.

★ ★ ★

The day of the baby's expected birth was fast approaching. My due date was 17 March 1981, St Patrick's Day, but in the meantime Brian had travelled with the team on Friday, 6 March to play against Halifax the following day. My last antenatal check at my doctor's had revealed a trace of protein in my urine and my blood pressure had risen, both common occurrences in heavily pregnant women. The doctor also noticed that my fingers and ankles were a little swollen. I was advised to go home and take it easy, advice that I stupidly ignored as I carried on cleaning and shopping and all the rest. My ankles were a bit swollen. So what? Life has to go on.

My next check on 6 March was at the hospital and the story could not have been more different. By now, my blood pressure had shot up so alarmingly, I was told I must be admitted immediately and they weren't taking no for an answer. I must say, I didn't feel especially unwell. Still, my mother was now with me, so she was sent home for my overnight things and I was put straight to bed. I was in the grip, I subsequently discovered, of eclampsia, a potentially fatal toxic condition.

Instead of being confined to bed, or maybe because I wilfully disobeyed instructions, I made it my business to try and track down Brian in Yorkshire. He'd left me the number of the hotel where he was staying, but it was now the middle of the night and I couldn't get through. These were the days before mobiles. I was the only patient on this large ward, and the two nurses on duty were sitting in the kitchen chatting to each other rather than keeping an eye on me. I must have spent an hour standing in the corner, on the phone, becoming more and more frustrated as my efforts failed to produce results. My legs started to ache and I developed a blinding headache. I went to see the nurses who ticked me off, gave me some tablets and put me back to bed. Then all I remember is drifting in and out of consciousness.

The next four days were a complete blank. I had two fits, apparently, before Amy was delivered by emergency Caesarean section — the only option left open to the doctors if my life was to be saved — at around three o'clock in the morning of 7 March. One piece of good fortune, though, was that John McPherson, the consultant on duty that night, specialised in obstetrics and he took the decision to take me straight into the operating theatre, rather than waiting to see what happened. I'm convinced to this day that he saved my life.

As it was, I had a third, more serious fit after the baby had been delivered. I was quite unaware of all this, of course, or of Amy's removal to a specialist care unit in Exeter. The medication I'd been prescribed to reduce my blood pressure had been absorbed through the umbilical cord by my precious daughter. She needed urgent monitoring.

Brian was eventually alerted and was driven by taxi through the night from Halifax to Torquay, the football club generously picking up the bill. On arrival at the hospital, he was greeted with the news that the baby was fine, but in Exeter, and that the doctors rated my chances of survival at no better than 50:50. His first sight of me, he later told me, stopped him in his tracks. I'd blown up like a balloon and had tubes coming out of me everywhere. The next few hours were to prove crucial. If I had another fit or my kidneys failed, I'd almost certainly die.

My first memory, after I regained consciousness four days later, is of being shown a Polaroid photograph of my baby, and being told it was a girl. 'Oh, but it should have been a boy,' I blurted out, but only because I was convinced I'd been carrying a boy and that a son would be nice for Brian; they could have played football together. That same day, Amy was returned to the hospital in Torbay, although she was still in an incubator because she'd developed jaundice. I loved her straightaway, but I was still very weak and I hadn't the energy somehow to feel that fierce, instantaneous bond that's meant to take place between mother and child.

My first image of her will never fade. She looked just like me. Her hair, sparse as it was, might have been strawberry blonde — much more like her father's colouring — but her features were mine; they are to this day. Because of her Caesarean birth, she wasn't in the least wrinkly like most babies. She weighed just under six pounds, and when I held her in my arms, she seemed to me just beautiful, perfectly formed.

I was in hospital ten days in all and my father and sisters came to see me. Amy was his first grandchild and their first niece.

Everyone was thrilled with her, even my father. The story made the TV news bulletins and the front page of the newspapers. I've still got all the cuttings. Then Amy and I were allowed home. I tried breastfeeding her for about two weeks, but it was hopeless, so I gave up and expressed my milk into a bottle. She cried all the time and then developed colic, screaming non-stop from six to nine every evening without fail. That went on for the first three months of her life! For the first few weeks, though, I had my mother with me, so I was able to get some rest through the night when she or Brian would feed Amy. He was fabulous from the start, a real hands-on dad, and yet he was only twenty-three when she was born. He was always taking her off me so I could have a rest and begin to regain my strength.

Amy was a shocking baby! She didn't sleep through the night until she was two, but I had the constant support of a loving husband and that made all the difference in the world, and when she wasn't crying she was smiling at everyone and was a total delight.

Less than a month later, my sisters went on a promotional tour of Japan where the Nolans were riding high. At one stage, they were more successful there than The Beatles, selling over nine million records throughout our career. Each sister, Coleen included, came back and banked a royalty cheque of £50,000 for Japanese sales, a great deal of money in those days and something, I must admit, that made me a bit jealous. I'd sung on 'I'm In The Mood For Dancing' and 'Don't Make Waves' but I'd missed out on this major payday, and Coleen hadn't even sung on those two big hits. On the other hand, that Japanese tour was gruesome, I'm told. There'd be five or six TV appearances a day and then live shows at night. I hadn't been involved in the hard graft of making those records such big hits in Japan. Anyway, I had my prize and it was something on which you couldn't place a price. I could hold my own precious baby in my arms. I happily settled down to longed-for motherhood.

Amy was a year and a half when a travelling fair came to town and we decided to take her. I was trying out my shooting prowess at one stage with Brian standing behind me, Amy in his arms. As I fired the gun, a tiny piece of metal flew out of the rifle and straight into Amy's eye. She screamed — and so did I. Luckily, Brian took control of the situation and drove us to the hospital in Paignton as I nursed a sobbing Amy in my arms.

The doctor did his best to remove the fragment of metal from her eye, but she was crying so hard and wriggling around so much, he had next to no chance of success. It was decided she'd have to have an anaesthetic which immediately panicked me, but it was the right decision. The metal was removed without any lasting damage.

Unfortunately for my sister Maureen, though, she saw a news report before she heard the happy outcome from us. Maureen is Amy's godmother so, when she arrived at Heathrow, having been on holiday, the newspaper hoarding proclaiming: 'Nolan baby shot in eye' sent her running to the nearest phone. By the time I picked up the receiver in Torquay, she was in floods of tears. I'll never forget her relief when she discovered that all was well.

On another occasion, when we were still living in Paignton, I had taken Amy to the football; we went every Saturday to watch Brian play. At the end of the match, I strapped her into her car seat and joined the queue to leave the car park. Some youths from the opposing team — they'd lost the game — spotted Amy with her little Torquay United hat and scarf. I don't suppose it was any more than a bit of mischief, but they suddenly started rocking the car from side to side. It must have seemed funny to them, but it felt very frightening being inside the car and especially with a vulnerable toddler. I was shouting for them to stop. Amy was crying. It was scary, especially when they started banging on the windows. Then a policeman spotted what was happening and told them to move on. That incident also got into the papers.

★   ★   ★

The Nolans, meanwhile, were given four TV specials, which I used to watch with a whole swirl of different emotions. I loved Brian and I'd have laid down my life for Amy, but I'd look at the screen and think that it could have been me up there singing along with them. But the mood would quickly pass. I couldn't have been happier playing the role of wife and mother.

Their musical director by this stage was a chap called Robin Smith. He and Coleen were living together although she was still only sixteen and he was only a few years older. I didn't disapprove, but I couldn't help feeling that her life, the freedom she had, was very different from when I was her age. The fact that she had independent money, of course, meant that our father had no real control over her. She could afford to do what she wanted and that's exactly what she did. I kept in constant contact with all my sisters by phone and they with me; they were all mad about Amy and would ring for almost daily bulletins on her. Whenever they had a free day, they'd come and visit me.

Unbeknown to me, Robin had written a song called 'Amy', inspired by my daughter, and the girls had included it on their latest album. I switched on one of their TV specials one evening and the girls started singing the song, accompanied by a succession of photographs of me and Amy on the screen. I still remember some of the words:

I don't think that anyone could ever know
The happiness you brought when you came into our lives
Amy has a thousand words she wants to say
And maybe Amy knows we love her as she plays
As the years go by
I hope she realises
There is no need to ever be sad
'Cos Amy will give you all the love we have

I sat there, crying my eyes out. I didn't want to be back with them full-time, but I wished

I'd been there for that special song.

Then they appeared at the theatre in Paignton and I took Amy along. She can't have yet been two at the time but, at the end of one of their songs, they invited me to bring her up on stage. I also went to see them with Amy when they were appearing in Fowey in Cornwall. I walked into their dressing room and they all stripped off naked in front of me as they changed into their stage outfits. It took me by surprise. When I'd been part of the group, we'd never have done that! But now they seemed completely natural about it. They were living life at a faster pace and they had to change at high speed between songs.

It was shortly after that visit to Cornwall that I experienced one of the greatest shocks of my entire life. Each of my sisters attracted fans who fastened on to them alone — and I was no exception. Although I'd bowed out of the group because of Amy, there was a young girl — I don't think she was yet twenty — who had a bit of an obsession with me. She was slender with mousey, shoulder-length hair and a slight West Country accent. She lived in Plymouth and I think she identified with a Nolan who also lived in Devon.

She'd write to me and she got hold of my phone number so she'd ring me, too. She even turned up at the house on a couple of occasions. She once brought a little tricycle as a present for Amy. She became a bit of a nuisance in that she began writing on a regular basis and then she'd be upset if I didn't answer every letter. I'd sense an antagonism when she wrote the next time, asking me why I was ignoring her, but the truth was, she wasn't a friend; she was a fan. She seemed a little lost, a bit strange, someone with no real life of her own. I was nice to her, though, and, because of that, I think she built it up into something more than it was.

I was at the hairdresser's one day and I'd taken Amy with me. I spent more time there than usual and then I decided to do a bit of shopping in Torquay, so I'd probably been away from home longer than I'd told Brian. While I was out, he received an anonymous phone call — presumably from this young fan — warning him that Amy was going to be kidnapped. Naturally, he immediately rang the police who took the threat extremely seriously. Brian tried to reach me at the hairdresser's and was told I'd left about an hour ago. Now he was frantic while I was blissfully unaware of all of this, wandering round the shops with Amy in her pushchair. An hour after I was expected home, this had turned into a major alert. Police were combing Torquay and Paignton, looking for me and Amy. By the time I eventually got back, Brian was standing anxiously at the door.

I was surprised to see two detectives in the house. They sat me down and started firing questions at me. Where had I been? Had anyone suspicious approached me? Was Amy all right — and so on. Then they told me why they were so concerned. And that's when the colour drained from my face. They asked if I knew of anyone who might have some sort of grudge against me. I told them that I couldn't think of anyone, but I did mention this rather obsessive fan who I was gently trying to discourage. Maybe she was fed up and had seen this as me giving her the total brush-off. So they took the details and went to check her out. As it turned out, it had indeed been her. Poor girl, she ended up being sectioned and placed in a psychiatric unit. That was the last I heard from her.

That incident apart, I was content with being a wife and mother. I honestly loved housework and shopping and looking after Amy. Brian was doing fine at the football club, although we were finding it hard to exist on his wages and keep up with the mortgage repayments. I wasn't receiving any royalties from sales of singles recorded after I'd left the group, and I certainly hadn't saved any money from when I was singing with my sisters. We borrowed money from his dad and my sister Bernie. I felt quite comfortable with that; they were family, after all, and the Nolans were on the crest of a wave. In the last couple of years, they'd had five Top 20 hits.

With hindsight, it might have been more sensible if I'd found a job in Torquay or Paignton, but what could I do? I didn't know anything else except singing. I'd left school when I was fourteen so I had no qualifications. As our financial struggle intensified, it was pretty obvious where the answer lay. Brian and I sat down one day for a serious financial conversation. He'd seen me crying when my sisters had sung the song called 'Amy'.

He said, 'Do you want to go back to the group?'

I was honest with him. 'I cried,' I said, 'because yes, I miss my sisters and singing with them, but also because of the words in the song. I'm terribly torn. I don't want to leave what you and I have here.' I paused. 'On the other hand, we do need more money. What do you think?'

'It's up to you,' he said.

I wasn't worried about the physical demands of being part of the Nolans again, but I did find the prospect daunting for other reasons. They'd had a string of hits in the meantime which I would have to learn. They were big stars now with their own TV specials. I'd be part of a much more successful act than the one I'd left. Also, I knew that a return to my show business life would take me away from the two people I loved more than anyone in the world, but there didn't seem any real alternative.

There was the question, though, of how this would impact on Amy. She was only nineteen months old. Brian wasn't going to give up his football so there was only one solution: Amy would come with me when we were on the road, but with Mum travelling with us to look after her when we were performing. If we were busy with TV work, my mother would stay in our house in Paignton with her; or Amy could stay with her in the house in which my parents still lived in Ilford. As soon as I put this to her, she agreed immediately without even consulting my father. She loved the idea of seeing more of Amy.

So I called the girls. It was Maureen who answered the phone.

'What would you think,' I said, 'about the

possibility of me coming back into the group?'

Initially, I think she was a bit surprised. 'Well, we'd have to have a meeting about that,' she said. 'You're absolutely sure, are you? It's no good coming back and then wanting to leave in a year.' I could tell that she was slightly worried how my other sisters would react and I understood that. I assured her, though, that I was deadly serious. Two hours later, she rang back. 'That's fine,' said Maureen, 'and we're all one hundred per cent behind you.'

Now that I had to go through with it I felt a whole mix of emotions, including being quite scared. Had I done the right thing? But there was no going back. I couldn't let my sisters down. So it was settled. In October 1982, almost exactly two years after I'd left the group, I was once again one of the Nolans. Now I'd just have to get used to stripping naked in front of them!

10

On the Road Again

Early in 1983, Robin Smith wrote a new song for us. 'Dressed To Kill' jumped straight into the charts at number 35, our quickest entry ever. It was obviously going to be a big hit, so our record company decided we needed a new image. We were given elaborate hairstyles, strong make-up and dressed from head to foot in leather and lace. You certainly couldn't miss us! It was utterly different from our previous altogether more homely appearance.

In fact, so striking was this new look — lots of attitude, no smiles — that it was decided to give away a poster of us all in our fancy gear with each record sold. Although this later became common practice throughout the industry, it was totally new back then and frowned upon. Unbelievably, the people who controlled the charts arbitrarily 'demoted' our record to number 95, a position from which it never recovered. We all felt pretty hard done by.

The girls had first gone to Japan in 1980

when I was pregnant with Amy and had left the group. They'd performed at the Tokyo Music Festival and Stevie Wonder was one of the guests. I'd always been a big fan and was sad not to have met him. Then, in 1983, the Nolans were invited back. It was a long way away and we'd be gone six weeks. I'd miss Brian and Amy almost more than I could say, but I was part of the group again and I had to honour our professional commitments.

While we were in Tokyo, we were booked to appear at the Blue Note jazz club. By coincidence, Stevie Wonder was touring the country at the same time and, as luck would have it, his end-of-tour party took place in the club. After we'd completed our act, we were invited to stay on and join the party. He arrived after everybody else, and in real life he looked exactly as I'd seen him so many times on screen, except I was surprised by how tall and slim he was. We were introduced to him. He had such a nice, gentle, unassuming manner. He even agreed to pose for a photograph with us; I've kept it to this day.

There was a piano on stage and, without prompting, he sat down and started playing all his hits. It was like a private concert, like sitting in his front room, quite unforgettable. Every time we asked for a special request — 'Isn't She Lovely?', 'Superstition', 'For

Once In My Life' — he'd play it. He's so talented that his voice sounded just like it did on all his records. It was like being caught up in a dream. It seemed almost surreal, an experience I'll never forget. Even so, nothing could compare with getting home and seeing Brian and Amy after being away from them for so long. I almost physically ached to hold her in my arms again.

We were still hugely popular in our native Ireland and toured there again for two weeks later that year. I'd been feeling a bit unwell and then I had a nasty fall when I tripped over an iron bar during rehearsals in an Irish TV studio; I was thrown up into the air and landed heavily on my back, bruising my right hip. It shook me up more than I realised. The comedian Roy Walker was also on the show and he walked me back to my dressing room.

Never mind the bruise. What worried me was that I'd just discovered I was pregnant again. I'd already told Brian our good news, and I'd confided in my sisters who had been incredibly supportive, never allowing me to pick up anything heavier than a teacup. Nor was there any animosity about my rejoining the group and then having to take a break when the baby was born. I had quickly reassured them that I'd be happy to work almost up to the birth.

As it turned out, it wasn't to be. I stayed with my parents in the house in Ilford the day we returned from Ireland, but I was keen to get back to see Brian in Torquay. I told my mum that I was feeling a bit queasy and she persuaded me to stay the night with her. My father had slowed down quite a bit by this stage. It was 1983 and he was in his fifties now. He seemed to have mellowed into middle age and appeared genuinely concerned about my welfare. Even so, I'd look at him sometimes and that dark secret would come unbidden into my mind. It was a legacy I was never going to be able to eradicate completely.

The following morning, I insisted on going down to Devon, but by the time I got off the train in Torquay, I was suffering sharp pains in my stomach and they were getting progressively worse. Something was obviously wrong and Brian called the doctor. The pain was excruciating and I'd started to bleed. I knew from my first pregnancy that I was suffering a miscarriage. The doctor gave me a shot of morphine straight into a vein which stopped the pain instantly, and then he called for an ambulance. At the hospital, a scan revealed that I'd lost the baby.

I remembered my first miscarriage and the feeling almost of relief that accompanied it.

This was different. The last time, I was the unmarried eldest daughter in a Catholic family with a burgeoning career and a thoroughly wholesome image. Now I was married and very much wanted a brother or sister for Amy. Nor had I been scared of another pregnancy, despite Amy's rather dramatic entry into the world. There was nothing to suggest that I'd suffer in that way again. I'd cried the first time I'd miscarried, precisely because I felt guilty about not having to face the problems that would ensue had the baby been born. This time, I went numb with the loss. I had no tears to shed. Naturally, Brian was sad about what had happened but he was more concerned about me and how I was coping.

I was kept in Torbay Hospital for two days which included having a dilatation and curettage operation before I was sent home. Bernie and Maureen came to Paignton to stay with me while Brian continued training. Then the phone rang after a few days. It was Norma, Brian's mum and a gentler creature you couldn't hope to meet. Her soft Geordie voice was in my ear. 'I'm so sorry, pet,' she said and the simple sweetness of her words cut me to my heart. All the pent-up emotion was suddenly released and I cried and cried for the baby I'd loved and lost.

★   ★   ★

Soon the demands of my career helped to take my mind off the miscarriage. It was at a post-golf tournament event, the Bob Hope Classic, that we met the great man himself. Each year, he hosted a dinner afterwards at the Grosvenor House Hotel in London's Park Lane. It was a huge black tie, ballgown affair held in the Great Room. President Ford was there — we had our picture taken with him — as were Princess Alexandra and her husband, Angus Ogilvy, alongside the rest of the great and the good. We received a massive cheer as we were announced, coming down the sweeping staircase into the Great Room.

With so much experience under our belts, we took most engagements in our stride, but this was different. We knew it was a prestigious event which was also being televised live. No wonder we were nervous. Backstage, we were all telling each other to keep calm. I remember saying to my sisters, 'If you do something wrong, don't stop. Just smile and carry on.' Then we rapidly rehearsed some of the trickier harmonies, something we rarely did on other occasions.

We were the cabaret along with Stephanie Lawrence who had been in both *Cats* and *Starlight Express*. Unfortunately, she slipped

205

on the stage and fell over, her skirt riding up over her head. The whole thing was really embarrassing. We felt for her, and it didn't exactly put us at our ease. Suppose one of us lost her footing or caught a heel in her dress? It didn't bear thinking about.

Suddenly, there was no more time for fussing and fidgeting. We were on. Bob Hope himself introduced us; a great thrill. We performed a Barbra Streisand medley, with Paul Williams, the man who'd written some of those songs — 'Evergreen', 'Watch Closely Now' — sitting right in front of the stage. It was that sort of an evening. We also sang 'People', 'Second Hand Rose' and 'Don't Rain On My Parade' from *Funny Girl*, and 'Woman In Love'.

This isn't meant to sound boastful but, vocally speaking, we didn't hit a bum note. Backed by Alyn Ainsworth's orchestra, it was one of the most accomplished live performances of our career. We were continually being rubbished for being cheesy but we could sing and nobody ever said otherwise. I'm very proud of that evening.

Even allowing for the excitement of that engagement, we all had the feeling that perhaps the Nolans were beginning to peak. The hit singles were drying up and, while we still got bookings, they weren't quite as plentiful or as prestigious as they had been in the glory years at the end of the seventies and the beginning of the eighties. In November 1983, Linda announced she wanted to leave the group to pursue a solo career. Her husband Brian, who'd been our tour manager and had assisted the sound engineer, obviously would go with her.

Linda's last performance as part of the group was the *Val Doonican Christmas Show* on which Howard Keel and Wall Street Crash were the special guest stars. We had a particular affinity with Val because he used to sing with my Aunty Doreen, my dad's sister, back in Ireland. He's also the nicest man in the world, everybody's favourite uncle, relaxed, highly professional but always calm about everything. Most of his shows went out live; not that you'd have known it to look at him. Nothing seemed to faze him.

It was a real thrill to be on the same show as Howard Keel because he'd long been an icon of ours. We all loved his big movie musicals — *Kiss Me Kate, Seven Brides For Seven Brothers, Calamity Jane* — so it felt as if we were rubbing shoulders with Hollywood royalty. His voice was still fantastic and he was such a masculine man. You'd never have known, though, that he was a major star. He sat on the sofa next to us and chatted away like a long-lost friend. Like Sinatra, he had no need to appear big; he knew how good he was and had nothing to prove.

If I was concerned that the dynamics of the group might change with Linda's departure, I needn't have worried. Initially, it felt a bit strange going from five people to four, but we quickly readjusted. We also redistributed the different harmonies and ended up sounding pretty much the same as before.

Early in 1984, we were booked to appear on Marti Caine's TV show. We'd already done a special with her, so we knew what a star she was to work with. I think we felt an additional affinity because we were now Blackpool-based and she was a northern girl from Sheffield. She'd worked the clubs before she won the *New Faces* talent competition and there was absolutely no side to her. Everyone remembers her as a comedienne, but she also had a great singing voice. After battling bravely, she finally succumbed to cancer in 1995. She was a great loss.

The remaining four of us then recorded a new album, *Girls Just Want To Have Fun*, and undertook a highly successful promotional tour of Woolworth and Asda stores. This was followed by yet another tour of the UK, performing in theatres and clubs, although by now we were no longer topping the bill. I've always liked a live audience better than, say, the endless repetitive work in a recording studio. Amy would come with me, my mum babysitting her while I was on stage.

Poor Brian was back in Paignton and still playing. He was captain of Torquay United by then, but the old injuries to his knee and ankle were giving him a lot of pain. We were separated more than I'd have liked because of my work. He'd always take me to the station to see me off on yet another engagement or tour, and I'd look out of the window as the train pulled away from the platform and watch his solitary figure making for the exit.

We were then booked for an appearance on Little and Large's TV show. Like Marti and us, they came from the northern club scene, so we immediately shared a kind of shorthand. Not only did we sing, but we did a comedy sketch with them — well, they did the comedy and we fed them the punchlines. They told us they originally got together when Syd Little had been doing a stand-up routine and Eddie Large started heckling him. In the end, Syd said, if he thought he could do better, why didn't Eddie come up on stage? So he did — and their double act grew from there.

We still see Syd — he lives in Fleetwood,

the next town to Blackpool — but we've never really kept up with other people in the business. We're not standoffish but we're sisters, and so we always had each other's company, which meant we never got to know the other artists apart from what was required through performing with them. I've always been close to Maureen because she's only three years younger than me and we grew up together. Having said that, it would be hard to fall out with Maureen. She's placid and kind and the opposite of confrontational. Coleen's just the same; anything for a quiet life. If I crossed swords with anyone, it was Bernie. The trouble is, I suppose, that we're too alike. Each of us can be fiery. I remember coming off stage after one show and I could see she was angry with me.

'I couldn't hear myself singing,' she said, 'because your voice was so loud in my ear.'

'Me too loud?' I exclaimed. 'I couldn't hear myself singing because of your bellowing.' And so we'd start bickering. I'm perfectly prepared now to admit that I was probably short-tempered because I wanted Amy and me to be at home with Brian.

Christmas 1984 was very special because we were invited to perform for a week at the Diplomat Hotel in Bahrain. Everyone came: Mum, Dad, both brothers, all the sisters, boyfriends, Amy and me — everyone, that is, except for Brian. December is bang in the middle of the football season and there simply wasn't a choice. That's show business, as they say, and, in our different ways, we were both in it, but I know he was lonely that Christmas, with Amy and me on the other side of the world, and I missed him dreadfully. We spoke on the phone every day, as the enormous bill proved when it arrived a few weeks later. It wasn't an ideal existence and I never got used to missing Brian. If there was just a day's break in our professional diary, I'd travel back to Torquay to be with him.

I liked singing with my sisters but I also liked and needed the money. Brian and I had never lived lavishly — we never once went on holiday while we lived in Paignton — but I do remember we got into the habit of eating out quite a lot, and we did choose to pay for Amy to go to a private nursery.

Looking back now, I can see it was a schedule fraught with possible problems, an accident, if you like, waiting to happen. And it did. We girls were staying in Ilford for a couple of days — there must have been a brief break in the tour — and I was up early one morning because of Amy. There was a huge teapot in the kitchen because there could be up to eight of us in the house at any one time. I made tea and sat Amy on the worktop next to me so I could keep an eye on her. I leant across to reach a cup and in that moment she must have been attracted by the tea cosy because she pulled at it and the pot overturned, emptying its boiling hot contents.

None of it spilled directly on her but the stream of scalding tea flowed across the surface, seeping under her bare legs. The first thing I heard was a blood-curdling scream. Immediately, I grabbed her with both hands, dumped her in the sink and turned on the cold-water tap. Then I wrapped her in a blanket, ran upstairs with her and woke my mum, screaming, 'Amy's been scalded! Amy's been scalded!'

I knew she needed urgent medical attention and my dad got up and drove us to the hospital in Ilford. I held Amy in my arms. She was in shock, gently moaning the whole time, and it wasn't hard to know why. I looked at the back of her legs. The skin was peeling off in front of my eyes. It was like a living nightmare. I was convinced she'd be scarred for life.

At the hospital, one leg was bandaged from ankle to thigh, the other from ankle to knee. Then every so often, I'd have to take her back there to have her blisters burst and the wounds re-dressed. I was always full of trepidation, but Amy seemed to accept what was happening and was incredibly brave throughout the whole procedure. She hardly ever made a fuss or cried. My guilt at what had happened reduced only slightly when a doctor told me that my swift action of running cold water over the burns had almost certainly prevented Amy from suffering permanent scarring.

⋆ ⋆ ⋆

When Brian was twenty-seven, he got injured again and decided his playing days were over. For a season, he was hired as the team's assistant manager. Football had been his life, but he knew his career was coming to an end and it hit him hard. One day, he announced he wanted to return to live in Blackpool. Although I'd been away a lot, I'd loved the four years we'd been in Torquay — it wasn't called the English Riviera for nothing — but I didn't resist the idea of moving back north. All my family were in Blackpool, even my parents — they hadn't yet sold the house in Ilford, but they had recently moved back — and Brian's parents were in Newcastle. Amy would be starting school quite soon. In

213

Torquay, we would have had to employ someone to look after her if I was away and Brian had continued as assistant manager of the team. In Blackpool, there was a whole support system on hand to collect her from school and so on.

For six months, we stayed in my parents' house in Waterloo Road. It was a testing time, and we usually preferred to stay in our room when we weren't out looking for a house of our own that we liked and could afford. Although my father never again made any sexual advances towards me, I was never truly comfortable in his company. We never discussed it, but instinctively neither Brian nor I let Amy out of our sight while we were living there. We certainly never intentionally left her alone with my dad, which is such a sad thing to have to acknowledge. I'm pretty certain he wouldn't have touched his own granddaughter in an inappropriate way, but merely having to consider such a possibility in relation to your own father demonstrates the way in which the legacy of sexual abuse — and this had taken place more than twenty years earlier — can continue to throw its shadow over innocent lives.

Brian was the sort of man who'd turn his hand to anything. He was very practical and would have happily taken a job in the building trade, but there was no work going. Then he started playing, just for fun, for a local amateur football team run by a man who owned a commercial estate agent's. He knew Brian was looking for a job, so he offered him one on the insurance side of the business, working with his brother. It wasn't fantastic money, but I know he was pleased to be bringing home a wage again, even though he wasn't the type of man to feel threatened by his wife earning more than he did.

By that stage, we'd found a three-bedroom semi on Falmouth Road in Blackpool, not far from my parents and my brothers and sisters. We'd both liked it the moment we walked through the front door. Nor did we have to do anything to it. It was newly decorated in a style I didn't want to change and there was a little garden at the back which was nice for Amy and safe, too. We got her into a Catholic school a walk away from where we lived and close to my parents' house, so that my mum could pick her up from school if Brian was at work and I was on tour.

Although the hit singles were now a thing of the past, we were about to have a chart-topper as part of a charity record. On 11 May 1985, Valley Parade, Bradford City's football stadium, caught fire and fifty-six fans lost their lives with over two hundred more

215

injured. Fronted by Gerry Marsden, more than a hundred stars recorded a new version of 'You'll Never Walk Alone' to raise money for the families of the victims, and it immediately went to the top of the singles chart. I wasn't able to break open a bottle of bubbly, though, for one very good reason.

On the last leg of yet another British tour, we found ourselves in Lowestoft, and as we were about to start the gig, I began to feel unwell. I put it down to tummy ache and joined my sisters on stage at eight o'clock. Two hours later, the ache had escalated into something much more painful. By the time I got back to the hotel room I was sharing with Maureen, I was being sick, so she called a doctor, who diagnosed indigestion. He gave me some tablets and an injection to stop the vomiting. It did the trick, but only temporarily. The sickness returned a couple of hours later with a vengeance. We were due back in Blackpool for a few days' rest before travelling to Scotland for the final leg of the tour, but I never made it home. At Lowestoft Hospital, suspected appendicitis was diagnosed.

I insisted my sisters stuck to their itinerary; nothing was to be gained by them staying with me. I had an operation to remove my appendix and just in time, it seems. I was told that, if I'd made the journey back to Blackpool, I'd have run the risk of peritonitis setting in and that can be fatal.

Once I was strong enough to leave hospital, my father drove to Lowestoft to take me home. I would so much have preferred it if it had been Brian, but I accepted he had a living to earn. As it was, I deliberately lay on the back seat of the car, pretending I needed to sleep because I didn't want to talk to Dad. I hated being in that small, confined space with him. He was being perfectly nice to me, but I couldn't get out of my mind the memory of when we'd been in another car all those years ago and he'd suggested we could run away together.

I quickly resumed work, both at home and overseas. The tours were getting further and further away. In the end, my sisters went to Australia three times (although I didn't accompany them the first time in 1983 because that was when I'd bowed out of the group to be a wife and mother), as well as to Japan and Russia. It was exciting going away at first, although I pined for Brian and Amy. Then, after a bit, all the tours sort of blurred into one. We'd arrive somewhere, the sound system would be checked, we'd do our performance and then move on the next day to somewhere else. It was a strange existence because you never really got a proper sense of where you were. However, the audiences were always enthusiastic, which makes you feel appreciated, and the money was good. I always felt the same: six weeks is too long to be parted from the two people you love best in the world, but singing with my sisters never stopped being fun. As ever, I was being tugged in two directions.

One trip does stick in the memory, though. We toured Russia for six weeks in 1986. We were part of a cultural exchange. The UK got the Bolshoi Ballet; Russia got the Nolans. I think the UK probably got the better end of the bargain! It was an extraordinary experience, but I found it particularly hard being so far away from home because it was so difficult to find a phone with an international line. I felt more cut off than ever from Brian and Amy.

There were thirteen of us on the tour: Maureen, Bernie, Coleen and me plus our four-piece backing band and a road crew of five. We all got on with each other really well and that included me and Bernie. There wasn't much alternative. We were in a strange country sharing the same adventure. It was like stepping back in time to the last century: very rural, very primitive. I remember looking out of the bus window and seeing a woman tilling the land by hand with a ploughshare. Everything seemed to be beige or brown or black. I never saw any bright colours. Food was sparse — we seemed to live on little more than boiled eggs, cheese and cucumber — and there were no shops in the way that we were used to in the West. Everywhere you went, there were queues, and we were constantly approached by people who wanted to buy our jeans, bags, belts, CDs, you name it.

We played in giant stadiums seating anything up to 10,000 people and they were always full to capacity. In Tbilisi, Baku, Azerbaijan, the story never varied: a total sell-out, but it wasn't because we were hugely popular in Russia — as a matter of fact, we were hardly known there. It was because people were starved of Western culture and were eager to satisfy their curiosity by coming to see us perform.

I remember one leg of the tour when we had to transfer from Baku to Leningrad. The coach trip would probably take twelve hours, although we four girls had airline seats booked for a flight that would take no more than three hours. However, Coleen and I hated flying, so we gave our tickets to two members of the band and decided to travel with the rest of them in a pretty battered old bus with no toilet facilities. We made sure we packed sandwiches and bottles of water — just as well in the circumstances as we never saw anywhere en route that sold snacks.

In time, of course, we were all dying to get off the bus for a toilet break, but we didn't see any signs for a public lavatory. Eventually, we asked the driver — through our interpreter — to pull in at a small village off the main road. The interpreter approached a house, knocked on the front door and got permission from the owner to use her facilities. We were then led through the house and into the garden which was overrun with a horde of children. The owner was sitting there with a baby on her lap. She indicated a makeshift structure covered in sacking. This was the toilet. Coleen and I looked inside. There was a hole in the ground surrounded by planks of wood covered in old excrement and flies swarming everywhere. It was absolutely disgusting and almost certainly a health hazard. Coleen decided she could hold on and got back on the bus, but I just had to relieve myself so I gritted my teeth and got on with it. I emerged as quickly as possible, convinced I'd probably have picked up typhoid or dysentery in the process. Then I noticed a stream running along the bottom of the garden. Perhaps if I rinsed my hands in the water, I'd reduce the chances of contracting any infection. When I got back on the bus, I said to Coleen that at least I'd been able to wash my hands — and the crew started howling. I asked them what was so funny. 'Because we've all just peed in that stream,' piped up one of them. After that, I felt unclean until I reached Leningrad and was able to scrub my hands with soap and hot water.

There was little opportunity for us to have a social life in Russia because there weren't any clubs we could go to when we'd finished our act and, anyway, we were always on the move. Any downtime was spent in one of our bedrooms where we'd play cards, drink vodka, put on some music and have a laugh. On one particular night, we were staying in the largest hotel in Moscow — bigger than any in Europe. It was so big that each floor had its own reception area. Suddenly, there was a knock on the door. There stood the floor receptionist and she ticked us off in broken English, telling us to turn off the music and return to our individual rooms. We apologised and promptly disregarded her instructions as soon as the door was closed again. Half an hour later came another knock. Again, the hatchet-faced receptionist was telling us off, only this time she was accompanied by a soldier with a rifle that he was pointing directly at us. Strange, isn't it, how persuasive someone can be from the other end of a gun?

11

Arrivals and Departures

Brian and I never discussed how often my work took me away from home. I felt self-conscious about it. Yes, I always missed my husband acutely, but *I* was the one off on the adventure, singing with my sisters, entertaining audiences. *He* was the one stuck at home on his own. I knew he minded.

Just before I'd go off on another trip, we'd perform the same little ritual.

He'd say, 'I miss you.'

'I'm not gone yet,' I'd reply.

'I know,' he'd say, 'but I know how I'll feel when you have and I miss you already.'

Of course, if he'd ever once said that he'd prefer me to leave the group, that he'd rather I were at home with him all the time, I'd have quit the Nolans without hesitation. However, money was always an issue, and so the subject was somehow swept to one side. Perhaps, too, Brian didn't want to put me in a position where I had to make the decision regarding whether or not to end my career.

As it was, I often had Amy with me so his

loss was twofold, but there was a level of deep trust between us — there had to be — without which the marriage couldn't have survived. Now and again, I might mention to friends, tongue in cheek, that I hoped Brian behaved himself in my absence. Without fail, the answer was always the same and music to my ears. He never talks about anything else but you, I was told. It was all the reassurance I needed.

In the spring of 1986, the girls and I went to Australia (my first trip) and Tasmania. Sydney was everything I'd hoped it would be, a magnificent city on the sea with the opera house dominating the harbour, but, if anything, I preferred our time in Tasmania. We were performing at a major sports centre in Launceston and staying in a hotel on the complex. We were in the pool every day and then doing the show each evening for a week.

It was like a holiday except I didn't have Brian and Amy with me. I'd phone home every day — sometimes as many as three times — which again meant that I had an enormous phone bill to pay at the end of it all. The trip was as good as it could be. It could never be perfect, though, because I missed them both so dreadfully, but I mustn't be dishonest. I didn't only agree to make the trip for the money, such as it was. The fact of the matter was that the opportunity to go to Australia might never happen again and I'd always wanted to see it for myself. As usual, I was being pulled in a number of different directions.

I love travelling, but I hated having to walk away from my husband and, when I went abroad, my daughter, too. And yes, the money would come in dead handy. So what a shame it wasn't more! We'd been away for six weeks and, I suppose, after all the expenses had been deducted for our musical and crew support, we girls probably received about £300 each a week. This is not a complaint because it was a wonderful experience, but I think most people would imagine that chart-topping artists criss-crossing the globe would be fabulously wealthy as a result. That simply wasn't the case, even though £300 over twenty years ago was worth quite a bit more than it is today.

Not long after we got home, we were booked for a summer season at the Bournemouth International Centre, and Cannon and Ball were top of the bill. It was a fabulous summer. We rented a beautiful house in Bournemouth and all got along really well with Tommy, Bobby and their families. When we weren't working, we'd regularly get together for a barbecue and to

225

play rounders or tennis. Bobby Ball and I became particularly good friends and, as show business people often do, we'd always give each other a big hug each time we met. On one such occasion, Amy, who was with me throughout the summer, saw Bobby throw his arms around me. She was five at the time and not used to seeing any man other than her dad hugging her mum. It must have made an impression on her because, the next time she was on the phone to Brian, I heard her telling him what had happened.

Brian arrived in Bournemouth the next day. God only knows the torment the poor man must have suffered on his journey. What he expected to discover when he arrived in Bournemouth must have been tearing him apart; he had a very long face when he got to the house where Amy and I were staying. It didn't take a minute, though, for me to put him right. We hugged and kissed and he was soon all smiles again. I could tell how relieved he was, and when, later that day, he came with me to the theatre and Bobby gave me a hug like he always did, Brian could see how innocent it all was. In the end, something good came out of what could have been something bad. Because of the misunderstanding which had brought him to see me, he was then able to stay for two days and we had a wonderful time.

Brian's job working in insurance was full-time and I was often away on singing engagements. This meant Brian could take Amy to school in the morning, but we sometimes relied on my mum to pick her up in the afternoon and babysit her until one of us could come and collect her. Each of us made a particular point of only ever asking my mother to look after Amy in our absence, never my father, and I never intentionally left Amy in his sole care, but, on more than one occasion, I'd call round to collect her and Amy would be there with my dad. That immediately worried me.

I'd say, 'Where's Mum gone?'

And he'd reply, 'Oh, she wanted to go and play bingo, so I said I'd keep an eye on Amy. Why, what's the problem?'

My heart would stop, but my father would just stare at me, daring me, I felt, to voice what possible objection there could be. I never did. Why didn't I say something to him on his own? That question haunts me to this day.

The fact that my mother would decide to go out was proof, I believe, that the thought of her husband abusing his granddaughter never crossed her mind. But it had crossed mine. I'd later ask Amy, apparently casually and in all innocence, if anyone had ever touched her or done anything to her she didn't like.

'For instance, has anyone ever touched your private parts,' I'd ask, 'one of your uncles, maybe, or your granddad?'

She'd always say no, of course not, but, if I ever found her at my parents' house with just my father, I'd have to question her about what might have happened. I worried about it all the time, and yet Brian and I didn't really discuss it properly. He only ever said one thing on the subject. We were lying in bed one day and he turned to me.

'I think you ought to go and see a psychiatrist,' he said. 'I think you need to deal with what your dad did to you.'

'But that was a long time ago,' I replied. 'I've lived with it for years and years now. It's long past.'

He didn't say anything else, but I realise now that what he was really saying was that, as I'd never confronted my father about what I suffered at his hands, counselling of some sort might lead to him being made to answer for his actions.

As it was, I think both Brian and I were not only frightened of opening a wound that might never heal, of causing a rift that could tear the family apart, but also of no one believing my story. If these horrible things had happened, why had it taken me this long to make them public? And how would I have explained to Amy that she couldn't be left at my parents' house in case my father started sexually abusing her? I appreciate that her safety should have overridden all of this, and yet still I remained mute. I've thought about this so many times down the years and I've tortured myself with why I let the situation drift on when something could have been happening to my precious daughter. In my defence, I was as insistent as I knew how to double-check that both my parents would stay in all evening if they were babysitting Amy — and mostly they did. This may sound like clutching at straws and in many ways it was. But the longer I didn't say the real reasons for my concern, the more I couldn't.

I'm certain that my father never did lay a finger on Amy, but what was I thinking? I felt I couldn't tell my mother what was on my mind because I'd decided all those years ago that I had to live with this terrible guilty secret. Anyway, if I had blurted out what I knew to be the truth, my father would have dismissed it as fanciful nonsense — something he might have convinced himself was true, for all I knew. I thought of asking Aunt Teresa to babysit Amy in future but, again, what possible reasons could I keep inventing that explained this decision to my mother? She'd have been mystified and terribly hurt.

What I should have done, of course, is taken my father to one side and told him that he was never to babysit Amy alone and that he knew exactly the reason why. I can't come up with a reasonable explanation as to why I didn't. I don't offer this as any sort of an excuse, but I was still frightened of him. He had the sort of personality that had always struck fear in my heart. I don't remember feeling like that about him before he started touching me, but, when he did and I gradually came to understand how wrong it was, it forced me to reassess him. I thought I'd known my dad and I hadn't. He was this other person with a dark side that wasn't natural. It coloured my whole view of him. He'd become like a stranger who could behave in an unpredictable way and do vile things to me.

In the meantime, if ever Amy was going to be looked after by my parents, I stressed as vehemently as I knew how that I wanted my mum to be there, I wanted *her* to be the one who tucked Amy into bed, I wanted *her* to stay at home throughout, in case Amy woke from a bad dream and needed a reassuring hug. Anyway, I told myself, with rather more conviction than I truly felt, perhaps I was worrying about nothing — but the sins of my father, it seemed, continued to cascade down the generations.

★ ★ ★

In the November of 1986, Maureen, Bernie and I were travelling home to Blackpool on the M6 after performing a gig in London, and we reached Shevington, near Wigan, at about 6.30 in the evening. Bernie was driving with Maureen sitting next to her and me in the back. It was dark and raining heavily. I was leaning forwards, chatting to my sisters. At that time, it wasn't compulsory for rear seat passengers to wear a safety belt. I have no recollection of what happened next, only that when I opened my eyes Brian was at my hospital bedside.

I later discovered that a motorcyclist had lost control, skidding from the nearside lane across both carriageways and into our path. Bernie's reactions were good and she managed to stop in time before hitting him, but the motorway had been busy with commuter traffic and the car behind ours must have been too close. In the slippery conditions, it rammed into the back of us with several more following suit. It's a wonder that nobody was killed.

Bernie and Maureen suffered whiplash injuries and delayed shock. I was severely concussed with a bad laceration across my forehead just above my right eye. It required thirteen stitches. Apparently, my only complaint was of a headache. The cut was jagged and could quite easily have left an unsightly scar but, by a stroke of good fortune, the surgeon in charge of dealing with my wound had just returned from the Falklands where he'd had plenty of practice sewing up all too many serious injuries. He did a wonderful job.

A couple of months later, our album *Tenderly* was released. Of everything we ever recorded, I felt this was the one with the most potential. It was a collection of standards, and we were each allowed to pick our favourite tracks for inclusion. I chose 'I Get Along Without You Very Well', 'As Time Goes By' and the Ella Fitzgerald classic 'Every Time We Say Goodbye'. The problem was, we didn't build in enough time in the studio, with the result that I've always felt we could have done a better job. Really great albums can take as long as two years to get just right; this was recorded in two weeks.

In January 1987, I discovered I was pregnant again. I was thirty-six and both

Brian and I were keen to produce a brother or sister for Amy who would soon celebrate her sixth birthday. There had been one other miscarriage along the way but, unlike the second one at three months, this had been at no more than three weeks. I'd been working with my sisters in Amsterdam when I'd started to bleed profusely. A doctor was called and quickly established that I was suffering a very early miscarriage. Naturally, it left me feeling low but, since I hadn't known I was pregnant in the first place, I experienced far less grief than before.

Now, though, I was pregnant again and this time — I was determined — it was all going to be just fine. Even so, my gynaecological history was such that Brian and I told each other we mustn't build up our hopes too high. Every precaution was taken to ensure I took no risks whatever that could endanger this precious pregnancy. As before, my sisters wouldn't allow me to carry anything, and during rehearsals, they insisted I sit down as much as possible. They generally wrapped me in cotton wool.

We'd recently signed a six-album contract with National Panasonic to record popular Japanese hits, but with new English lyrics, for release in Japan where we were still riding high. The English translations of these lyrics were so bizarre that we had trouble singing them because we kept getting fits of hysterics. Even so, that album, and the ones that came after it, all sold well in Japan.

This was the same year that we were part of a second charity record, a reworking of The Beatles' 'Let It Be', with all the funds going to the families who'd lost loved ones in the Zeebrugge ferry disaster. Paul McCartney (who'd written the song in the first place), Mark Knopfler from Dire Straits, Boy George and Kate Bush all sang on the record. There was very little socialising, although we did have a drink and a bite to eat afterwards. I remember chatting to Boy George who was lovely, very flamboyant, very witty, but, to be honest, I think we were a little overawed to be surrounded by so many famous faces, most of whom seemed more hip, more fashionable than us.

Our next tour was of our native southern Ireland, although we also went to the north as well. I remember feeling a bit anxious. Would audiences in the north take against us because we came from the south, or those in the south because we'd moved to England? Then there was the political situation. There were soldiers with guns in Belfast as well as on the border with the south which seemed very sad and strange. Happily, any doubts I might have had about how the audience would respond were dispelled as soon as we started performing. I can honestly say that the reaction in Andersonstown, for instance, was as good as we'd ever known anywhere in the world.

This was the first time we'd been back to Ireland since we'd started having hits in the UK Top 20. In Dun Laoghaire, we performed in a large pub where the punters were literally hanging off the rafters. People were fighting to get inside to see our act. The conditions were pretty basic: we had to change in caravans, I remember, because there were no dressing rooms, and no toilet facilities except in the pub. We couldn't very well fight a way through the crowds in our costumes to go to the loo, so Bernie and I peed in pint mugs and threw it out of the window!

We were fortunate that our summer season that year was to be in Blackpool at the famous Opera House. Cannon and Ball were again topping the bill and a young, up-and-coming comedian, Brian Conley, was also in the show. Brian was no stranger to us as he and his band, Tom Foolery, had supported the Nolans once before and we'd become good friends. I was under strict instructions, as my pregnancy progressed, not to join in any of the choreography. In fact, a joke was made of my condition and I did all my singing from the comfort and safety of a wrought-iron garden chair.

★ ★ ★

Our second daughter, Alex, was born on 18 October 1987 in Blackpool Victoria Hospital. Two days before her arrival, I'd started suffering stomach pains, and as a precaution, I was ordered into hospital. Mild labour pains continued until about eight hours before she was born, at which point everything started in earnest. Because of Amy's traumatic entry into the world by emergency Caesarean section, I had no experience of acute labour pains. Oh boy! But, as any new mother will tell you, the moment you hold your baby in your arms for the first time, the pain instantly becomes a distant memory.

I'll never forget letting Amy hold Alex for the first time. She gazed and gazed at her and then said, 'Hello, I'm Amy, your big sister.' So sweet. Once again, Brian rose to the occasion of new fatherhood with his customary loving attention. It was just as well because, for some reason, I was taking longer than I'd have liked to get over Alex's birth.

Two weeks after her arrival, we decided to have her baptised, part of a dual christening with her two-year-old cousin, Tommy, son of my brother Tommy, grandson of my father Tommy. (It's an Irish tradition!) The day went really well although I was aware of a sort of dragging feeling in my legs. I put it down to tiredness after the rigours of labour. The following day, though, I was presented with the explanation. I'd gone to the bathroom to use the bidet when I suddenly felt I urgently needed the toilet. Before I could move across the room, I felt as though I was on the point of giving birth all over again, although this time without the accompanying pain. When the feeling passed, I looked down into the bidet. There was a blood clot lying there the size of a side plate. I struggled to my feet and phoned for the doctor. 'Touch nothing,' she said. 'Cover it over. I'll be there straightaway.' True to her word, she was at the house in minutes. After examining the clot, she explained that it was part of the placenta that must have been missed at the hospital.

With the extreme anxiety of Amy's birth, three miscarriages before Alex's safe arrival, and now this latest episode, Brian put his foot down.

'I've made a decision,' he said. 'I'm going to have the snip.'

I asked him why.

'Because you had a terrible time with

Amy's birth. You've just been through this trauma with Alex. You've had three miscarriages. We've been blessed with two beautiful daughters. I love you and I'm not prepared to stand by and put your life in danger ever again. Enough is enough.'

I might have dreamt of a large family, but Brian was adamant. Part of me was sad that Alex would now be my last child but, on reflection, I think it was the right decision.

★　★　★

Six months after the birth, I gradually started returning to work but, luckily, we travelled less during 1988. This was also the year both Maureen fell pregnant by her partner Ritchie, and Coleen by her first husband, Shane Richie. We cut back on travel and tried to confine ourselves to television work. We appeared on Rod Hull's TV show, for instance, and managed not to get savaged, as Michael Parkinson most famously had, by the vicious Emu. But we did get our bums pinched!

We also guested on Lena Zavaroni's show. She seemed sad somehow and yet she should have been happy: she'd realised her dream by winning *Opportunity Knocks*, her career was going well, the public clearly adored her. But who knew what demons were tormenting her? Eleven years later, at just thirty-six, she was dead, the victim of long-time anorexia nervosa and, ultimately, bronchial pneumonia. So tragic. She'd been an only child. It made me realise how lucky we were to have each other.

At the end of 1988, I decided to tackle my first pantomime. Linda and Denise were seasoned panto performers by now, while Bernie had two to her credit. As a family, we'd always tried to keep the Christmas holiday free of work but, when I was offered the part of Robin Hood in *Babes in the Wood* with Les Dennis, I admit I was tempted. When I was told it would be at the Theatre Royal in Newcastle — Brian's home city — it seemed to have my name on it. Then I was told how much I'd be paid. No contest! I was on £1,200 a week for eight weeks, the most money I'd ever earned. What's more, I'd be able to stay with Norma and Walter, Brian's parents, and Alex could be there with me. Amy would remain in Blackpool with Brian because she had to go to school.

There was to be just a fortnight's rehearsal, during which I had to learn the art of sword fighting. My opponent, the evil Sheriff of Nottingham, was played by Basil Soper. We must have looked like David and Goliath.

Basil is over six feet tall and almost as wide. I didn't come up much above his chest and there was nothing of me. I also had to learn how to use a bow and arrow convincingly. For both skills, I was taught by Jonathan Howell who was cast as one of my band of merry men, but his chief role was that of stunt coordinator. Without him, I wouldn't have been able to tackle either task.

On opening night, kitted out in a little green jacket and hat, my legs encased in nothing but tights, my feet in stiletto-heeled boots, I concentrated on not looking daft while also summoning up the spirit of Robin Hood, best bowman in the land. The target was set up on stage in full view of the audience. I picked up my trusty longbow, loaded an arrow and slowly brought the bow down in front of me to train it on the bull's-eye just as Jonathan had taught me. A hush fell over the audience as I drew back the string. I released my grip — and the arrow fell to my feet. Cast, musicians and audience gasped as one and then everyone rocked with laughter. I was mortified. It must have been first night nerves because it never happened again. Most nights, I hit the target; on a good one, I got the bull. The local paper wasn't kind, though. Their critic said I was the worst principal boy ever to have trodden the boards

240

of the Theatre Royal. He was absolutely right!

We were a couple of weeks into the show when it became apparent that Norma was finding it hard to cope with Alex who was now an active fourteen-month-old toddler. Norma wasn't strong physically: she was a diabetic with only one kidney and she'd recently suffered from a hiatus hernia. Alex was also a drain on her emotionally: she would become very clingy before I left the house for the theatre each day and then she'd sob when I was gone. Norma was feeling increasingly stressed and hated seeing her granddaughter so upset. Brian and I talked through the options and decided in the end that Alex ought to be with her sister in Blackpool, although it did mean he'd have to manage both the girls on his own.

A few weeks later, Brian brought them up to Newcastle to see the pantomime. I put out my arms to take Alex from him, to give her a cuddle. Although she came to me, it was with some reluctance and it was clear she wanted to be back with her dad. It was a horrible feeling for me to realise that, because she was so young, the few weeks she'd spent with Brian and away from me had been sufficient for her almost to forget me.

In later years I would never find it easy being away from home over the panto season, and particularly while the girls were caught up in the magic of Santa Claus. I always insisted, though, on travelling home — from however far away I might have been — so I could spend Christmas Eve and Christmas Day with Brian, Amy and Alex. It was so lovely waking up in my own bed and spending Christmas with Brian and the girls.

That first pantomime season, we met up with the rest of the family for Christmas dinner which we celebrated by taking a private room in the Savoy Hotel in Blackpool with our own bar and waitresses. We stayed for hours, eating, drinking, talking and, of course, singing. Leaving home again on Boxing Day was such a wrench, but the money was good and we badly needed it following my enforced break after Alex's birth when I wasn't working. Brian, though, was still bringing in regular money from his job working in insurance.

The following Christmas I was in panto-mime in Liverpool, thankfully much nearer to home. I played Cinderella opposite Peter Howitt, famous for his role as Joey in the hit TV sitcom *Bread*. He was my Buttons and I don't mind admitting that, as the season progressed, I found myself growing more and more attracted to him. He was tall, blond, slim and very confident. We'd go for coffee together and chat for ages. He sang and played the guitar which I liked. On our opening night, he asked if he could escort me to the after-show party, but I turned him down.

'But the leading man traditionally accompanies the leading lady to the party,' he said.

'Well, not on this occasion,' I replied. 'You've got a girlfriend. I've got a husband. I'd feel awkward.' He looked at me as though I was mad, but I wouldn't budge, even though I fancied him. So I went to the party on my own.

I liked his style. For example, I confided in him during rehearsals that there was a particular song which didn't suit me and that I wished I didn't have to sing it.

'Well, tell the director,' he said.

'But I couldn't do that,' I told him.

'Of course you can,' he insisted, 'and if you get any trouble, just tell the director I said it was OK.'

So that's exactly what I did. Apparently, the director did go ballistic — but not in front of me. I only learnt about it afterwards — and Peter had stood up for me. He was very protective. The two men who played the Ugly Sisters would sometimes get a bit short with me if I didn't cotton on quickly enough about what I was expected to do and Peter would always pitch in on my side. 'Leave her alone,' he'd say. 'She's new to this. She'll get there in her own good time.'

During the second week of the run, Peter appeared in my dressing room one day before the show. We were chatting away and then we found ourselves kissing, a proper French kiss. It was lovely. I felt terrible afterwards, so guilty. It didn't stop me from doing it again, though, more than once. But kissing was where it began and ended. We never did anything more serious.

It was the only time in my marriage when I was fleetingly tempted to cheat on Brian. I never did and I never told him about Peter, although I think he suspected something might be going on. He turned up at the theatre one day, unannounced, with a small gift: a soft toy with the words 'Mad About You' printed on its stomach. There was clearly a chemistry between Peter and me which a number of people commented on when we were on stage together. However, I'd been propositioned a few times down the years, and I always resorted to the famous Paul Newman line, asking why I'd choose hamburger when I could get steak at home? This stood me in good stead. I loved Brian and he loved me. Why rock the boat?

Over the many years Brian and I had been

together, we'd never had the opportunity to have a proper summer holiday. We'd manage the occasional long weekend, or a few days when we could relax in each other's company, but the Nolans were always working a summer season each year and the winter had been hopeless for Brian because of his football commitments. However, in 1990, we decided to go to Disneyland, Florida, with the two girls, as soon as I'd finished appearing in a summer season split between Great Yarmouth and Skegness. We had to take out a small loan to pay for the trip, but I knew I had lots of work on my return and Brian was in regular employment.

We were all so excited as we headed off to Manchester Airport. We reached the front of the queue, loaded our luggage on the belt and handed over our tickets and passports to the check-in assistant.

'Do you have a visa?' she asked me.

'Visa?' Brian echoed.

'Mrs Wilson has an Irish passport. She'll require an entry visa to be allowed into the USA. Didn't your travel agent tell you?'

We were dumbstruck, but there was nothing to be done. Our luggage was removed from the belt and returned to us. We called for a taxi to take us home, with me crying and Brian vowing he'd sort something out with the travel agent. And he did. He was on the phone to them first thing the next morning and he stayed on it until the afternoon, by which time he'd discovered he could get a visa for me if he was prepared to drive to Liverpool and apply direct at the Irish Embassy. The travel agency admitted their error and got us four seats on another flight the following day. After the fraught stop/start, we enjoyed a magical family holiday.

My panto that Christmas was at Nottingham with Frank Bruno, by his own admission no Laurence Olivier. He was still UK heavyweight boxing champion at the time. I played Aladdin and he played the genie. I'd be in the cave, rubbing the lamp and waiting for the genie to appear. Before the audience saw him, suddenly that distinctive basso profundo voice would come out of the loudspeakers. They would erupt. 'Bru-no! Bru-no!' they'd shout. I'd have to stand there for at least a minute until all the commotion died down, and then Frank would appear through the floor of the stage — and everyone would erupt again. We'd then do a duet together, during which he always forgot his words and just started chuckling in that familiar way. It didn't matter. Everyone loved him. The Theatre Royal was full to overflowing every single night.

By the beginning of the nineties, the Nolans were still much in demand in clubs and bingo halls, but the music scene had moved on and we weren't having hit records any more. We always did a summer season, though, and there were overseas tours. In Japan, in 1991, we were presented with the Tokubstsu Kikaku Sho award, the Japanese equivalent of a Grammy, for best foreign recording artists. The previous year, we'd been given English lyrics to songs that had been popular for other artists in Japan and recorded them in London over the original soundtracks. It wasn't a bad idea and obviously the Japanese really liked what we'd done; hence the award. But you should have seen the lyrics! I still remember verses from two of the songs. The first was called 'Looking For Love' which included the following:

Look at his muscles on his u-huh
He's got legs that go up to his u-huh
Does he want to a-ha?
Course he wants to a-ha

Equally ludicrous was this:

A crazy fling

247

A moonlight dance
Next July, we fly to Mars
We run away from every day
As we play among the stars

I don't know what it was about the Japanese and the Nolans, but it seemed we could do no wrong in their eyes. The following May, we appeared on a BBC television show called *Noel's Addicts*, hosted by Noel Edmonds. The idea was that a member of the public was questioned on their specialist subject. On this occasion, the BBC had flown a young man over from Japan to answer questions on us. They were so obscure that my sisters and I didn't know the answers to most of them, but it wasn't a problem to the young Japanese guy: he answered every one correctly.

The previous year, we'd been delighted to be booked to perform at the Sandcastle, a famous swimming pool complex on Black-pool's south promenade, where Keith Harris and Orville were top of the bill. Keith struck me as a bit remote at that time and it wasn't until we later went on the road with him that I got to know the real man. He was kind and funny; he made us laugh all the time as he drove us from gig to gig.

Our brother Brian had recently married a

lovely girl called Lindsay, a dancer I'd worked with in panto at Liverpool. When Linda had left the group to pursue a solo career and her husband Brian had stopped acting as our tour manager, my brother Brian gave up looking after the merchandising side of our group and became tour manager. Lindsay was now working at a local private school, teaching dance and keep fit, but she agreed to help us choreograph some new routines for the summer show at the Sandcastle.

We'd been rehearsing for a couple of weeks with Lindsay and opening night was the following week, but Brian turned up one day to tell us that Lindsay wasn't feeling well enough to work. She was having trouble shaking off a heavy cold. The problem persisted, and then Lindsay started experiencing trouble breathing when she was lying down, so Brian called a doctor. He diagnosed a virus and prescribed a course of antibiotics. Two days later, when she'd failed to respond to the drugs and was throwing up black bile, the decision was taken to admit her to hospital, just as a precautionary measure, while they got to the root cause of her illness. She was well enough to get there under her own steam and yet, incredibly, devastatingly, she died two days later. She was just twenty-six. The diagnosis was that a massive viral infection had attacked her heart. The tragic loss of such a beautiful, vibrant young woman rocked everyone who knew her. Brian was beside himself with grief, utterly inconsolable.

It was well nigh impossible for us to get back to our work with any conviction or enthusiasm. The numbers Lindsay had choreographed were dropped from the show; their inclusion would have been too painful. Later on in the summer, and as a tribute to Lindsay, we did reinstate her dance steps, but they were a daily reminder of our talented sister-in-law, much loved, much missed.

12

The End of an Era

Towards the end of that summer of 1991, and after the tragedy of losing Lindsay, Amy, who was now ten, became ill. It started with her inability to keep any food or drink down. Initially, Brian and I weren't worried — children are often sick and then right as rain the next day — but the situation was complicated by the fact that Amy is phobic about vomit, hers or anyone else's.

The result was that she then wouldn't eat or drink anything, for fear she'd bring it all up again. I bought her all sorts of pops and cordials to tempt her. Eventually, she did drink one of them — and promptly threw up. She started to look terrible — drawn and deathly white — so we took her to the A&E department at Blackpool Victoria Hospital. A young doctor examined her and concluded it was no more than a viral infection. We returned home with Amy, much reassured.

The next day, she collapsed. We rushed her back to A&E and this time she was taken straight on to an emergency ward where a consultant saw her almost immediately. After a moment, he turned to me angrily. Why had I left it so late to bring her in? I explained about the previous day's visit and he gave the staff a severe dressing down for sending her home in the first place. Amy, meanwhile, was put on a drip and underwent any number of tests. It turned out that she was almost 50 per cent dehydrated. They kept her on a drip for a week.

Brian and I worked a kind of shift system so that one of us was always with Amy. After performing in the show at the Sandcastle, I'd go straight to the hospital where I stayed with her all night. Brian would be at home looking after Alex, and then he'd arrive in the morning and sit with Amy all day. The young doctor who'd originally examined her was full of apologies. As it was, she didn't suffer any lasting effects from her condition and after a week she'd bounced back to her normal, healthy self.

My professional life, although very different now from those years of being a pop star, suited me rather better. My sisters and I were able to accept individual invitations for one-off gigs, and spend much more time with our loved ones in between. Brian was still working on the insurance side of the commercial estate agency, a job he enjoyed although he hadn't got any qualifications at that stage.

We were still big in Japan, though, and made another visit there in 1992, mostly to promote our latest album. We did do one TV show which I shan't easily forget. We were rehearsing our song when we began to notice that all the cameras seemed to be very near to the ground. I whispered to one of my sisters, 'The viewers are going to be able to see right up our skirts.' It turned out, of course, that that was the precise intention. Without realising it, we were about to appear on a soft porn channel. As I was the eldest, my sisters elected me to go and complain to the producer, and he reassured us that the cameramen would definitely shoot us at shoulder height. So we resumed rehearsals and the same thing happened again. I marched up to the producer. 'Right,' I said, 'forget it. We're off.' They couldn't afford to lose us because the Nolans were so popular in Japan and eventually our contribution to the show was filmed the way we wanted it.

Back home, we did a summer season in Bournemouth with Joe Longthorne who did wonderful impressions of everyone from Barbra Streisand to Frank Sinatra. If you've seen — and heard — him impersonate Shirley Bassey, it's not something you forget.

He was lovely to work with, although he never socialised with us; he wasn't a family man so I think he preferred keeping his private life just that: private. All the same, he's always very good to his fans. They're devoted to him. In fact, at the beginning of that season, no one was very interested in our act — they were there to see Joe — but I think we won them round. The same people would come to the show, night after night, sitting in the best seats in the house. It must have cost them all their savings but they seemed to enjoy the familiarity of it all. We'd also attract our own individual fans. Bernie and Maureen were probably the most popular, but Coleen had her own fans who liked her best and so did I. Mine were two men in their twenties who always made a beeline for me after the show.

In 1993, Coleen left the group, having given birth to a second son, Jake. Shane's career was going well, so she didn't need to work for the money, and anyway she wanted to be at home with her two boys. That left three of us. Bernie and I would still occasionally clash, but Maureen always kept the peace between us. This was also the year when the remaining Nolans started to become popular on the gay circuit. The audience loved an all-girl group with their matching outfits and choreographed dance steps. Our very first such engagement was at a club called G.A.Y. in the Charing Cross Road in London. The audience went wild, singing along to all the words of all our hits. I'd never seen anything like it. Some of them were even dressed like us! It was a scream. We absolutely loved it.

A year later, Bernie announced she, too, wanted to go solo. She said she'd particularly disliked performing in the bingo halls which we'd started to do when there was no other work. This time, Maureen and I really thought that it might be the end of the act. We couldn't see how just two people could hope to make the same sound once produced by five, and Bernie had probably been the most popular of the three of us. She was certainly the most vivacious, the best dancer and a strong singer with a mass of blonde hair and bags of personality.

Before she left, we did a summer season with her at the Grand Theatre in Blackpool and an appearance at the Frontier Club in Batley at the end of November, but easily the most memorable event also involved every member of the family with the exception of Denise who was on tour and Coleen who was at home while Shane was away, looking after their two young sons.

The centenary of the Grand fell in the summer of 1994 and, to commemorate the occasion, a variety show was put on. The Queen and Prince Philip visited rehearsals in the afternoon and we were all introduced to them, although they didn't attend the actual performance. The Nolan family were given the honour of closing the first half. Each member of the family was introduced to the audience and came on to the stage, one by one: Dad was followed by our brothers, Tommy and Brian, and then came Maureen, Linda, Bernie and me. Next came Mum and Amy and Alex, now thirteen and seven respectively, as well as Danny, Maureen's six-year-old son, who joined in with the rest of us.

We sang our version of Barry Manilow's 'One Voice' which began with my dad and grew as each member of the family joined in, culminating in all of us singing in harmony. I wouldn't want to seem big-headed, but I have to say the sound we made was tremendous. At the end, the audience erupted as one. It's an evening I'll take with me to my grave — but it was the end of an era. It had been twenty years since my sisters and I had transformed ourselves from being a Blackpool family club act into one of England's most successful female groups of all time. We'd conquered Europe and the Far East, winning more awards and accolades than I could count. We'd released eighteen singles in the UK and eight albums. There had been so many TV appearances, it sometimes felt as though we were on more often than the news. Now it was to end.

The Nolans were reduced to just me and Maureen. While we contemplated whether we had a viable future, we received an invitation to go to Japan to put some new harmonies on the tracks we'd recorded and to re-record some of the lead vocals. It was nice work, well paid, and I enjoyed the fact that, because there were just the two of us, we each had more to do. But what lay ahead, profession-ally speaking, when we returned to the UK?

We didn't have to wait long to find out. Back in Blackpool, we were approached by Nick Thomas and John Conway, who ran an entertainments company called Qdos which had put on a lot of our summer shows in the past. They suggested we hire two dancers and they'd guarantee us six months' work in Butlins camps and a summer show. So Maureen and I found two girls, Julie Payne and Lee Davies, who we took on to give the act a bit more spectacle, a bit more substance. Unbeknown to the audience, they each had a dead microphone to give the impression they were also singing; we'd broken the rule of a lifetime and recorded our sisters' harmonies on backing tracks to bulk out the sound, but the reality was Julie and Lee were hired for their dancing skills.

The four of us duly did a three-month tour of Butlins, a pretty soul-destroying experience. It all seemed a long way from the glory days of chart-topping singles and sharing the bill with an icon like Frank Sinatra. However, we followed that with a highly enjoyable six-week summer season with Tom O'Connor at the Riviera Centre in my old stamping ground of Torquay. We rented a house on the outskirts of town complete with what turned out to be a flea-ridden cat which caused Amy (of course!) to develop an itchy rash.

It was during that season that a man jumped up on stage and mooned at us, an event Maureen missed because she had her eyes closed at the time, having reached a soulful point in the song she was singing. As a matter of fact, I reassured her afterwards that she'd missed nothing, which makes it a bit of a mystery as to why the man felt so compelled to parade his bits and pieces in the first place.

It was also while we were appearing in Torquay that one day Maureen and I went to get some money out of a cash dispenser before going into a shop to buy magazines and birthday cards. She was at the other end of the shop, looking through the selection of cards and, as I turned round from the magazine rack, I saw a man approach her, slip his hand into her bag and take out her purse containing the money she'd just withdrawn. He'd been watching her and had followed her into the shop. He quickly turned around and walked towards the entrance, but I stood in his way. 'I'll take that,' I said and grabbed the purse off him. In hindsight, it was an impulsive and probably foolish thing to have done. He could have punched me or even pulled a knife on me, but I was so outraged he should have taken my sister's purse that I didn't stop and think. He was more shocked than me that I'd caught him in the act, so he just ran out of the shop. I then went over to Maureen who'd been completely unaware of any of this.

It was in the papers the next day — how I'd foiled a theft. I'd told a local journalist called Paul Levie what had happened and he'd written a story about what a heroine I'd been! Brian and I had originally got to know Paul when we lived in Torquay. He had his own small news agency and we'd become very friendly with him; in fact, Brian is godfather to his son. I remember he came to see me in hospital when Amy was born and my sisters were there. He started taking pictures and earned himself a tongue lashing from Maureen who, being protective, felt he was overstepping the mark, but when they got to know him better, they could see he was a nice man.

At the end of the year, Maureen and I did our first pantomime together at the Grand in Blackpool. She was Snow White and I was the Wicked Queen; it's much more fun being a baddie, and working with my sister dispelled any potential nerves. Because it was local, it also meant, of course, that we were based at home all over Christmas, a real treat. Alex, then eight, and her cousin Laura, Tommy's thirteen-year-old, auditioned for small dancing roles in the production and both were accepted, which made it a proper family affair.

Alex had already had a walk-on part in the stage musical version of *Summer Holiday* starring Darren Day at the Opera House in Blackpool. Both she and Amy had taken lessons at a local dancing school, but I can't say that either of the girls had expressed an interest in following me into show business generally or singing in particular.

The following summer, we did a tour — just Maureen and me, but we were used to it being the two of us by now — with The

Bachelors, Jimmy Cricket and The Grumbleweeds; we sang all our hits, a West End musical medley and we each had a solo. We followed this with a summer season in Weymouth but only had to work Wednesday, Thursday, Friday each week. We'd taken a house on the beach which meant we could laze around each day lying in the sunshine. It was lovely. Amy and Alex were there because it was the school holidays and Maureen's son, Danny, too. Brian came down for a fortnight; it was just a shame he couldn't be with us the whole time.

While I was away, he'd spend his free time helping to coach a local football team, Blackpool Rovers — he also played for them — and I'd go and watch the team play whenever I could. Later on, he coached other local teams: Fleetwood, Mechanics and Squires Gate. He just couldn't get football out of his system and it kept him fit. I regret now the number of football functions, company dances and so on that I had to miss because I was away working. I would dearly have loved to have accompanied him but, without my work, we couldn't have afforded the lifestyle to which we'd grown accustomed.

Having said that, money was never in abundance. If there were any gaps in our diary, I'd look for some work on my own. I remember once landing a gig in a local hotel just to boost our income, although I also wanted the experience of seeing what it was like performing solo. I borrowed my brother Tommy's sound system and used some backing tracks belonging to the Nolans. Accompanied by my friend, Dee Fitzgerald, who manned the tape machine, off I went. It was scary and a whole new challenge without two or three sisters to 'hide' behind, but I got a taste for it and, at one stage, I was doing two or three solo gigs a week.

In March 1997, Amy turned sixteen. We spent the day in Manchester on a shopping trip and then, in the evening, the rest of the family along with Amy's friends all gathered for a party at my parents' house in Waterloo Road. Dad hadn't been feeling too well during the day, apparently, but he'd decided to clean the oven using a strong abrasive cleaner, ignoring the printed instruction that he should use protective gloves and a mask and, rather more importantly, that the job shouldn't be undertaken by anyone suffering any kind of breathing problems. During the evening, he complained of feeling worse and took himself off to bed. He had been a lifelong heavy smoker, and it was the beginning of what turned out to be a year and a half of ill health. His breathing gradually deteriorated, the trips to visit the consultant at Victoria Hospital becoming more frequent. Within months, he was unable to go anywhere without an oxygen canister and a mask over his nose and mouth. My overwhelming feeling was one of pity. He cut an increasingly sad figure. He was only in his early seventies, but he no longer had the breath to walk the short distance to the end of the garden.

That summer, Maureen and I again appeared for a season with Tommy Cannon and Bobby Ball, but this time on a small tour of holiday resorts that included Scarborough, Skegness and Llandudno. On one occasion, we were joined in Scarborough by Amy and her friend Julia Duckworth who sang 'I'm In The Mood For Dancing' with us. They'd both just left school. I think Maureen and I were even more nervous for the girls than they were themselves, but they got through it and I felt so proud. Now my elder daughter had performed our greatest hit on stage. It was a milestone moment.

In October 1997, and without any warning, Brian's mother, Norma had a massive heart attack when she and Walter were driving in their car one day. They got her to hospital, but she never recovered and, in many ways, I don't think she wanted to. She once told me that she'd sometimes pray that she wouldn't wake up the following morning because she was always in pain. Brian was forty when she died and, although he has an older sister, Shirley, and a younger brother, Ian, he seemed to take it particularly hard.

Walter asked me to sing at Norma's funeral and I agreed at once. We chose an uplifting song called 'Going Home' and, as I sang it, I looked across at Brian. He didn't once meet my eye. He seemed lost in his own private world, blaming himself — and me, he later told me — for the fact he hadn't seen enough of his mother when she was alive. My being away would have presented him with the ideal opportunity to take the girls to see their grandparents. Once his mother had gone, he must have felt guilty, but for some reason he chose to shift some of the blame on to me.

Following Norma's untimely death, Maureen and I started working towards Amy and Julia becoming an integral part of the act. The first time we appeared for a whole show together was in Tenerife, at a golf tournament. We stayed for a week, they gave each of us a fabulous apartment and we only had to give one performance. Perfect!

The following year, the two of them appeared with us at a charity concert in

Blackpool. Their nerves weren't exactly helped when compère Jim Davidson, announcing they were about to join us on stage, urged the audience to pay particular attention to Amy. 'Look out for Anne's daughter,' he said. 'She's got great tits.' Nice one, Jim! Even so, and despite this somewhat crude introduction, Amy and Julia were an instant hit with the audience, a good omen for the future.

Nevertheless, I had mixed feelings about Amy taking up singing full-time. There's a lot of rejection in this business and, as her mother, I was naturally keen to protect her from that, but she was full of confidence by now and eager to pursue her career as a performer. The year came to a close with Maureen in panto in Weymouth and me in Southport. In the end, I appeared in eighteen pantomimes, only finally putting away my poison apple a couple of years ago.

During our first year together with Amy and Julia as part of the act, we did a series of summer shows everywhere from Weymouth and Torquay to Great Yarmouth and Weston-super-Mare. Initially, we'd been worried that the two generations wouldn't gel on stage — that Amy and Julia would make Maureen and me look like a couple of old bags! — but it worked surprisingly well. We adapted our costumes so that, if Maureen and I wore a particular type of top, Amy and Julia would wear a boob tube version of it and so on.

Later on, Amy and Julia and a schoolfriend called Laura entered a competition on Richard and Judy's *This Morning* programme. They had to sing down the phone to them and then they were invited to sing on air in the studio, but they were so nervous, they didn't get beyond that point. In time, they teamed up with another girl, Marie Claire, and sang at quite a few gigs in Blackpool, calling themselves 3rd Base. They looked and sounded terrific.

It was a shame they didn't carry on with it, but they became disillusioned. They'd been invited to London to make demo discs, something that turned out to be a bit of a con. They believed they were going to be offered recording contracts, that this was going to be their big chance, but they were just being used so that the producers could let an established artist hear how a song sounded. They were never paid for this work — and, of course, it came to nothing. The music industry has changed enormously since my sisters and I first started out, with all manner of technical wizardry now available to make people sound much better than they are, but Amy can genuinely sing well without any artificial help.

＊　＊　＊

One day, towards the end of the summer season of 1998, we got a telephone call. Dad had been admitted to hospital. He was now seriously ill. On our day off, Maureen and I travelled back to Blackpool to visit him. He was on a geriatric ward and, despite everything, my overriding emotion was pity. He looked terrible and so undignified. The ward was like a scene out of your worst nightmare. There were old people lying on their beds not properly covered up. Clearly, there weren't enough nurses to cope with the demands of the patients. At one point, my father spilt a cup of tea he was trying to drink and it went all over the sheets. I told the nurse, but nothing happened. So I went and offered to change the sheets myself. She said visitors weren't really meant to do that. But what was the alternative? She was rushed off her feet and Maureen and I didn't want our father lying in wet sheets. So, rather reluctantly, she let us do it. The next day, we went back to Weymouth. Then, three days later, came another call. Dad had died. The cause of death was given as progressive systemic sclerosis, a condition that attacks the lungs. He was seventy-two.

I woke Maureen with the news and then I

told Amy. Naturally, she was upset at the death of her grandfather and the tears flowed freely. Maureen started crying and then I did, too, but I wasn't crying for the loss of the father whose sexual subterfuge had cast a shadow over my life. I was crying because I was witnessing people I loved becoming visibly upset. My tears were for them. His death, if I could have confessed my true feelings, left me completely cold, but, equally, I felt no sense of relief. All the awful things he'd subjected me to had happened years and years ago and nothing would ever change them.

Although the season would have been over at the end of the following week, we felt we couldn't complete the tour and told our producers the reason why. Everybody was kind and understanding. We returned to Blackpool, where Dad was buried a few days later, following a service at St Kentigan's Church. It was packed. Alex read a poem composed by all the grandchildren; none of the rest of them felt strong enough to read it themselves, although they stood next to her. So did I, to show a little support and to give her a bit of confidence.

Then Maureen read the words of a Celine Dion song, 'Because You Loved Me', a special request from our youngest sister, Coleen;

again, she was too distraught, she said, to read it herself. Both my brothers, Tommy and Brian, said a few words before the coffin was carried out to be cremated. Mum was too upset to say or sing anything on her own. One of his favourite pieces of classical music, Debussy's 'Clair de Lune', was played as we filed into the crematorium with Frank Sinatra's classic 'That's Life' playing as the short committal finished. The wake was held at the Tangerine Club, a favourite of my father's.

A number of friends praised me during the day for my strength at holding my emotions in check. Truth be told, it hadn't been an effort at all. The funeral had little effect on me. When I'd seen my father at the hospital for what turned out to be the last time, I had told him — along with Maureen — that I loved him, but only because that was the expected thing to do. It really wasn't how I felt. And yet, despite the secret he and I shared, I tried to remember those carefree days in Ireland when he was good and life was uncomplicated. I reminded myself, too, that he could show great kindness, but what he did to me meant that I couldn't grieve for him when he'd gone. It was too big, too fundamental, an evil to overlook.

To this day, I believe he must have had a

split personality. Who in their right mind would sexually abuse their own daughter — and then carry on with the rest of their life as though nothing had happened? This is no defence of what he did, and it certainly didn't help me, but clearly he couldn't stop himself. My girls would say I'm making excuses for him, but I'm not. It's just that I'm keen that people should understand both sides of the man.

It is no exaggeration to say that my relationships with the opposite sex in general and my husband in particular were sullied by the memory of what I endured at my father's hands. Ultimately, that legacy contributed to the end of my marriage and threatened to cost me the unquestioning love of my daughters, the two people for whom I would lay down my own life.

Was he evil? Was he sick? Was he ill? I've turned those questions over and over in my mind more times than I can count, and I've at last come to the conclusion that they're irrelevant. My father did what he did and, all these years later and even though he's dead now, his actions still have the power to haunt and to hurt me. The abuser moves on. The abused has no choice but to carry the aftermath of the abuse with her for ever.

His death meant, of course, that he never

had to confront the consequences of his actions. He'd got away with it — and I resented that. I also resented the fact that I couldn't grieve for the father I should have loved. His actions had denied me what should have been uncomplicatedly happy memories of him. How could I ever think of him as a proper dad after what he'd done? When I was fourteen, fifteen, I'd go to bed each night and pray that, when I woke up the next morning, he'd be dead. I feel guilty saying that now and that, in turn, makes me angry. It's a vicious circle of negative emotions and none of it was my doing or, at least, not knowingly.

If ever he should come into my thoughts, even today, absolutely the first thing I think about is the sexual abuse he put me through. I've often wondered what I'd say if he walked in the room now. Would I confront him with the unforgivable thing he did to me? I'd like to think I would, just to try to understand his motivation, but he was a powerful man and I suspect I still wouldn't say anything.

⋆ ⋆ ⋆

My mother took a long time to get over the death of the man she'd known since they were both twenty. One day, I found her crying

271

in the kitchen. She started going on and on about what a wonderful man he was, what a fabulous husband and father. Suddenly I snapped. 'For God's sake, woman,' I said, 'he was a pig to you. He drank, he smacked you about, he womanised.'

She looked at me in a strange way. 'Yes, I know,' she said. 'Your father had another child, a girl, by another woman.'

I couldn't believe what I was hearing. It turned out the woman, someone my mother knew by sight, had been a girlfriend of my dad's before he met my mum. We kids knew nothing of any of this, but the woman had come to our house, apparently, and told Mum that our dad had made her pregnant. The baby girl was born in exactly the same month as my mother gave birth to Denise. I thought back to those countless occasions when my father had called me a tart or a slut, simply for smiling at a boy. I remembered, too, the time he'd denigrated my friend Jacqui in front of an audience because she — a married woman of two years — was pregnant. I could feel the anger rising in me at the hypocrisy of it all. One rule for him, one for the rest of the world.

So my father had been carrying on with someone else only a few years into his marriage. Denise was my parents' third child,

272

born just two and a half years after me in April 1952. To this day, she always maintains that my mother was harder on her than on the rest of us. Denise loved Mum unconditionally, but she sensed some sort of barrier between the two of them. Might that have been explained by my mother's mixed emotions around the time of Denise's birth? Certainly, Denise was closer to my father, perhaps closer than any of the rest of us.

For all that the simultaneous birth of my dad's illegitimate daughter must have hurt my mother dreadfully, she'd no more have walked out on her marriage than flown to the moon. And while his womanising had clearly tailed off as he'd got older, his drinking, if anything, had got worse. But couples soldiered on and weathered the bad times in a marriage back then; and I think that, despite everything he did to her, she never fell out of love with him. It does mean, though, that living out there somewhere there's presumably a middle-aged woman who's yet another Nolan sister. My brother Tommy did start trying to find her at one point not so long ago. He went on to the internet but it proved a fruitless search.

13

Letting Go

My parents had sold their house on Waterloo Road about a year before Dad died. They bought a bungalow, a walk away from where we all lived, which they felt would be easier for him with his increasing breathing difficulties. When he died, we organised the sale of the bungalow and moved our mother, now seventy-two, into sheltered accommodation under the supervision of a warden. We didn't like the idea of her being entirely on her own.

That seemed to be the right solution, but I'd drive by sometimes in the evening and I'd see her sitting at her window, staring out at nothing in particular and that made me sad. She loved TV. Why wasn't she watching it? I know the answer now: she couldn't concentrate on a programme because, to put it bluntly, she was losing her mind. We bought her videos and a mobile phone. We'd say to her, 'Mum, remember to take it with you when you go out, because then you can get in touch with us or we can get in touch with

274

you.' But she never did. 'I don't want to waste the battery,' she'd say.

On one occasion, I went round to her little flat and she had the electric kettle on . . . on the red-hot hob. There was smoke everywhere. It was only by chance that I'd popped in to see her when I did. I'd also turn up and find the cooker on — and empty. It would worry me silly. In time, of course, we had to move her into a care home. That was in 2005. Maureen and Coleen and I would take it in turn to have her to our houses for dinner. If she was with me, I'd ask if she fancied staying over. 'Oh yes,' she'd say, 'that would be lovely.' On one occasion she fell in the street and was confined to bed. That night, I prayed as hard as I knew how that she'd make a full recovery. Just the thought of her dying reduced me to tears. What a contrast to the way I reacted when we lost our father.

I still think about whether I should have told her about the disgusting things he'd done to me, but, in the end, I'm glad I didn't because it would have put her in such a difficult position. If she'd believed what I said, she'd have been faced with two stark choices: either to report him to the authorities and walk out on the marriage or to tell me to let bygones be bygones. Either way, she'd have been heartbroken. He wasn't a good husband, I know that, but as I say, she never stopped loving him even when he hit her if he'd had too much to drink.

By the time he was ill, of course, he couldn't have lifted a finger to her in anger although he could be verbally abusive to her. He was a tidy man but a hoarder, too. It drove my mother mad. On every surface, it seemed, there were little piles of my father's mostly useless possessions. One day, my mother went to move one of these piles and my father rounded on her.

'Why do you always have to move everything?' he said. 'Why can't you just leave my stuff where it is?'

I couldn't bear it. 'Well, if you didn't leave your stuff lying all over the place,' I said, 'Mum wouldn't have to tidy up after you. And don't you ever scream at her again.'

The words were no sooner out of my mouth than I felt awful. I looked at him with his oxygen mask and his canister and he struck me simply as pathetic. My words had obviously hit their target. He immediately slunk back to his chair. Even Denise, back in the days when we'd all lived together in Waterloo Road, felt the same as we all did when it came to his drinking. He'd arrive back from a football match and a heavy session in the pub and we'd all hold our breath. What mood was he going to be in? He might be full of jokes. He might be in a sarcastic, sullen frame of mind. Or he might be spoiling for a fight. You could never tell. If, by some miracle, he was sober, it felt like a wonderful bonus.

He was a complex, tortured man, someone with a terrible secret. Little wonder that I've never grieved for him. He's been dead ten years now but, if I ever think of him, any memories are tainted by what I endured at his hands. So no, I don't miss him, something I can say with no feelings whatever of remorse or guilt — and that's the only thing which does make me sad.

Years later, I told my Aunt Teresa all about it. I felt I wanted to share it with her; we're very close.

'Auntie,' I said, 'there's something I think you ought to know. I didn't wrap it up. I said, 'Soon after I first arrived in Blackpool, Dad started sexually abusing me.'

She began to cry. 'I wish I'd known at the time,' she said, 'because I'd have made sure he was sent to prison.' She was angry now. Then she said, 'Was there penetration?' So I told her, no. She got up from where she'd been sitting and came across and hugged me.

I said, 'Don't get upset, Auntie. The past is the past and it's best forgotten now. But I feel better for having told you.'

To this day, I still wonder why it took me so long to tell my friend Jacqui what had happened between me and my dad. I finally confessed a couple of years ago and she was both angry and a bit hurt, I think, that I'd kept it all to myself. It would have eased the burden to share my secret and she might have said something to *her* mum and then it would all have come out.

★　★　★

Maureen and I continued to perform with Amy and Julia, and we were asked to fill in for the final month of the summer season at the Grand in Blackpool. The Grumbleweeds had had to pull out when one of their number, Graham Walker, had to have an emergency triple bypass, so we were given a fifteen-minute slot. Amy and Julia were thrilled to be appearing in such a prestigious venue in their home town. We'd also do one-off corporate events as well as clubs, some of them on the gay circuit, summer seasons and then pantos every Christmas for me and Maureen and, later on, for Amy, too. However, television work had dwindled to little or nothing by then, and the offers of work were getting a bit sporadic, although, later on, we did get one job in Dubai which impressed the girls no end: we stayed in a magnificent hotel with its own beach; we went out into the desert and smoked one of those hookah pipes; we went shopping in the souk. It was fabulous.

Brian, meanwhile, frustrated at having no qualifications, sat all the necessary exams and set himself up as an independent insurance broker and financial adviser. He got work straightaway. All his previous clients followed him, not because he asked them to but because they liked dealing with him. By then, we'd remortgaged our house three times to release a bit more money. It wasn't that our lifestyle was especially lavish, but Brian didn't earn very much and, although I was pulling in more than him when I was earning, we spent every last penny and more, gradually slipping further and further into debt.

But I didn't realise the half of it. Brian was the one who knew about finances and I had left it all to him. I later discovered that he'd been summoned to court at one stage because we were behind with the mortgage and we were on the brink of having the house repossessed. He'd kept it all to himself. He was — and is — a very private man who bottles up his problems rather than sharing the load with someone else. While he was good with other people's finances, it seems that he struggled with ours.

I can't say I was angry when I eventually found out the size of our debt. So yes, we were in trouble, but that was no more his fault than mine, and he'd wanted to shield me from it. We were living beyond our means. Looking back, I'm pleased I didn't know about it, although it might have been a relief for him to have shared the problem, and it is possible that because I didn't know we were in so much trouble, I may have been more extravagant than I should have been. That might have been the point when Brian should have sat me down and explained the state of our finances. He'd needed £20,000 to start the business, £10,000 borrowed from a friend and the same amount as a loan from the bank. He used the bank loan to pay back the friend and then put up our home as collateral against the debt to the bank. Stupidly, as co-mortgagee, I'd signed the relevant forms — but then, I thought Brian knew what he was doing.

Later on, when he could no longer afford the rent for his office space, I paid to have our garage converted for him. I encouraged him to downsize in terms of his equipment; I pointed out that he really didn't need more than one desk, a couple of chairs, a filing cabinet and a computer, but the sad truth is that he never once set foot in this new office. I didn't know it at the time but, on reflection, I can see he was already in the grip of the early stages of his breakdown. Then the fates intervened in a way I could never have expected and Brian really began to fall apart in earnest.

★   ★   ★

In the intervening years since I'd first found a lump on my right breast, I must have had up to fifty cysts in both breasts. They weren't alarming because they weren't malignant. All that happened was that I had to go to my local doctor to have them aspirated — that involves a needle being stuck into the cyst to draw the fluid off, which doesn't hurt in the least. In March 2000, I discovered two more cysts in my right breast. This was such a regular occurrence, I simply shrugged it off.

On this occasion, I went to my GP who examined me and aspirated the cysts, but then discovered a third, deep-rooted lump which I hadn't detected. She said she couldn't aspirate it because she could tell it wasn't a cyst, so she referred me to the hospital where I had a biopsy. Brian was with me. When I was told I could get up and put

281

my clothes back on, I fainted. That had never happened before and I began to worry that this might be something more sinister. Back home, my breast felt tender and bruised and quite unlike any previous experience I'd had. I knew something was wrong although there were no other symptoms. I felt fit and healthy in every other way.

I returned to the hospital a couple of weeks later with Brian. The same surgeon asked me to sit on the bed in a cubicle. He put his hand on my knee, looked me straight in the eye, and came right to the point.

'I'm afraid it's cancer,' he said.

I didn't break down. I just asked him simply, 'What do we do now?'

He explained that I'd need an operation in the next two weeks to remove the lump but not the breast. Driving back home in the car, neither Brian nor I said much. I think we were absorbing the news in our different ways. But we're both very practical people. Brian had suffered a lot of injuries through playing football and his attitude was that you just got on with things as best you could, but when he did at last speak, he was tender and supportive.

As soon as we got home, I walked into the sitting room. Amy was there, waiting to hear how I'd got on.

'Well, what did they say?' she asked.

I didn't try and hide it. 'I've got cancer,' I said.

She said, 'Stop messing about, Mum.'

'I'm not,' I said. 'I've been diagnosed with cancer.'

I think because I was being so matter-of-fact about it, she wasn't as shocked as she might have been. She certainly didn't scream or cry.

Later on, when I felt she'd begun to absorb the news, I decided to have a more thoughtful chat with her. Alex hadn't yet got back from school. I was in the bath at the time — we never bothered with closing doors or locking them — and I called Amy to come into the bathroom.

'You know that cancer's a life-threatening disease,' I said to her, 'so I want you to be aware that I might die.' I've always spoken bluntly to the girls. 'I don't want you to be unhappy, though. Of course, I know you'll be sad — that's only natural — but please don't be sad for long. I'm almost fifty now. I've had a fantastic life. If it comes to it, I want you to think about that. I've had a better life than most people.'

And that was the truth. I'd lived more in the half-century I'd been on the planet than most people would have done in five lives.

That very year, the Nolans had been voted ninth best all-time girl group in a Channel 4 poll which was a pretty good achievement. Mine had been a great life. So I wasn't being callous or blasé. I just didn't want Amy to have any illusions about my getting well, imagining that everything would be all right. Of course, I hoped that would be the case, but it was far from being a foregone conclusion. I told Alex the next day as we walked back through Stanley Park where she'd been captaining her school netball team. I think I broke the news a bit more gently to her because she was younger than Amy — she was only twelve at the time — and it was a lot for her to take in. I tried to communicate the fact that cancer is a serious business but that mine had been caught relatively early and we all had to have a positive attitude about it.

When I told Mark Rattray — we were touring with him at the time — that I had cancer and was being admitted to hospital for a lumpectomy, he gave me the best possible advice. 'Right,' he said. 'Get in, get it out and get over it.' They call it tough love, don't they? But it's better than a lot of hand-wringing. There's nothing you can do about it so why not be positive?

I was admitted to the Victoria Hospital in

Blackpool on 4 April 2000 and had the operation two days later, on Denise's birthday, when the lump as well as a dozen lymph glands were removed. I was very sick when I came round from the anaesthetic — they put me on a side ward to keep an eye on me — but the good news was that the surgeon told me he hadn't found any evidence that the cancer had spread. It had been caught early, apparently.

Because the lymph nodes had been taken out, I had to do exercises to get back the feeling in my arm. Then I was told I'd have to undergo a course of radiotherapy; that was a necessity, it was explained, but I had the option of having a six-month course of chemotherapy first, if I wanted. It would improve my chances of beating the cancer, but only by a further 5 per cent. I didn't hesitate. I wanted to do everything to increase my chances of staying alive.

It was pretty horrible: it made me feel so ill after each session. We were booked to do a summer season at the Grand Theatre in Blackpool, so I had my hair cut short and also bought a wig — which thankfully I never had to wear, although my own hair did get very thin. I'd have a session of chemo in the morning, go home for a rest because it left me feeling so drained, and then go to the theatre for the performance each evening.

We were also doing Sunday concerts in Skegness. I did the first two or three of those, but it proved too much. I was feeling more and more weak and listless. At the hospital they did a blood test. My platelets were low and I had to have antibiotics pumped into my stomach as well as a blood transfusion. Luckily, Coleen had agreed to learn the harmonies and the dance steps for the act when I'd first been diagnosed. She lived in Blackpool so, when I said I wanted to drop out of the summer show for a couple of weeks through illness, she offered to step in for me. What's more, she wouldn't hear of taking my fee. She did it all for free because she knew I needed the money. I can never thank her enough for that.

Although Brian never missed one of my chemo sessions, I began to sense that something was wrong, either with our relationship or with him. He just didn't seem like the man I'd married any more. I felt he was distant and aloof. He'd be sitting in the room as I had the horrible chemicals pumped into me, he might be reading the paper, and I'd say something and either he didn't reply or he'd just nod. Something wasn't right.

One day, when I was resting in my bed, he sat on the floor and put his head in my lap. I

286

started stroking his hair. 'It'll be all right, Brian,' I said, with rather more conviction than I felt. At that stage, half of me thought that Brian's strange, abstracted mood was triggered by my illness, that he was worried I might not make it. Or that, at least, is what I told myself.

I know now that my condition was only part of the problem. Brian was also single-handedly shouldering all the worry over our desperate financial situation. What would happen to me? And to his job? And to the house? And to the girls? It was all too much for one person to cope with. So much was bottled up inside him, I'm surprised now that he didn't go off pop. The look on his face that day, as he sat on the floor, was just pitiful. He was a soul in torment, a haunted man, but I couldn't quite understand why. Of course, I only knew half the story.

The chemo sessions were over by September; I began the radiotherapy in October and finished it in November, just before my fiftieth birthday. At one point, my ex-brother-in-law, Shane Richie, rang me up. He'd heard I was in the wars and wanted to offer some help. 'Look, if you want to go private, just tell me,' he said. 'Whatever you need, I'll pay for it.' He couldn't have been kinder and he didn't tell anyone else he was making this offer. It was such a shame that he and Coleen didn't go the distance. They seemed so suited to each other, like peas in a pod. They were born in the same year, just one day apart, and they had such similar personalities. Still, they're each happy now with their new partners.

I only found out very recently that Brian had been going to surprise me with a trip to Disneyland in Florida with Amy and Alex; and then I'd got ill. As it was, we had a birthday party at a local restaurant in Blackpool for family and friends. Brian was supposed to be arranging it, because I was still having radiotherapy sessions and I was a bit out of it — but so, in his different way, was he. As people started arriving, it became clear he hadn't organised it properly and hadn't booked enough places, so there weren't enough seats for everyone to sit down. That was so unlike Brian, up until that point such an orderly person. It was as though he was losing the plot.

The following March, in 2001, a plan emerged for the whole family to go to Florida. There was my brother Tommy, his wife and two kids; me, Brian, Amy and Alex; Maureen and Ritchie with their son Danny; my brother Brian with his current girlfriend; Denise and her partner Tom; Bernie and her husband Steve and daughter Erin; my mum and Aunt Teresa; Coleen and her two sons, Shane Junior and Jake — the three of them stayed in the house she owned in Florida; and a few friends, too. Only Linda and her husband Brian didn't come on the holiday because they'd very recently been to Florida. I'd also persuaded my friend Jacqui and her daughter to come along, too.

For some reason, I thought that inviting Jacqui had put Brian's nose a bit out of joint which I felt explained his slightly moody behaviour. It was as if he wasn't there. We'd go to one of the theme parks and I'd suddenly notice he'd gone wandering off. It wasn't just me, either. My sisters started commenting on Brian's absences when the rest of us were enjoying ourselves — he never seemed to be around — and then on his strange, dislocated mood when he was with us.

Amy celebrated her twentieth birthday while we were in Florida, so we arranged a party by the pool and an opportunity for her to swim with the dolphins. I was arranging all these treats, completely unaware of the true state of our finances. No wonder Brian was so preoccupied. I can see now that he was on the verge of a nervous breakdown. It was also on this trip that my mother started behaving out of character. What we didn't spot was that this was the early onset of Alzheimer's; we thought she was just getting a bit eccentric.

One evening, Denise, Maureen, Bernie and I stayed up after the others had gone to bed. We'd had a few drinks and we started talking about Mum and Dad. We were laughing about some of our mother's recent behaviour and then we moved on to our father who'd been dead by this stage for three years. It was Maureen, I think, who said he'd also been pretty eccentric in his own way.

'Eccentric?' I said. 'I wouldn't exactly describe him as that.' And then I found myself blurting out the whole story of my sexual abuse. It was the drink talking. The three of them just sat open-mouthed as it all spilled out. They simply couldn't believe what they were hearing. Shock and incomprehension gradually gave way to anger although it wasn't directed at me. They saw me, quite properly, as a victim.

'What did he do?' asked Denise.

'How long did it carry on?' asked Maureen.

'Did he ever say sorry?' asked Bernie.

I tried to answer all their questions as best I could. But, in the end, I told them there was nothing to be done about it. He was beyond reach now. I'd lived with this secret for so long that I must admit it was a tremendous relief and release to unburden myself. We were all in tears by the end of that long night.

Denise, Maureen or Bernie must have subsequently told Tommy and Brian, perhaps it was on that same holiday, because in time I came to realise that they knew. I then tried to talk to each of them about it, but neither wanted to know. Brian found it difficult to hear a bad word about him. Tommy, however, was clearly discomfited by my revelation. Any time I brought it up, he'd mumble a few words and wander away. I think he felt a kind of guilt that he should have known something was happening and done something about it, but I would hate him ever to feel he'd let me down. When I was being abused by my father, Tommy was the last person I wanted to find out, with the exception of my mother. In my confused state, I thought he'd think less of me if he discovered what had been happening and I was pretty sure he'd all but kill our dad. So the one person who might have been my saviour was the very person from whom I was most anxious to keep my secret.

One of my sisters must also have told Coleen because she referred to it a little later. She cried when she was told what had happened but, because she was the youngest and because she'd stayed in Blackpool when most of the rest of the family, including Mum and Dad, had moved south to pursue our career, the influence of our parents on her was much less pronounced. By the time she was in her midteens, she was part of a successful group and living away from home with her boyfriend. My father had always had less influence on her, not least because she left home at sixteen.

Linda and Brian hadn't been on holiday with the rest of us in Florida. Shortly after we got back home, they came to dinner with me and my Brian. After the meal, we were sitting around chatting about work and family and our childhood. Then we moved to the subject of my father, recalling how he'd been very much the one who ruled the roost. 'He always liked to be in control,' I said.

My Brian suddenly piped up, 'Why not tell them what else he got up to?' I'm sure this wasn't much more than the effects of a bit too much alcohol but I was shocked. Brian was putting me on the spot and without in any way having warned me first that this was what he was about to do.

Everyone stopped talking and I could see the blood draining from Linda's face. 'What do you mean?' she said. 'What else *did* he get up to?'

So I told her. As soon as I'd finished, she ran out of the room upstairs to the bathroom.

She was there for ages. Eventually, her Brian said to me, 'I think you'd better go and check on her.'

I went up and found her sitting on the edge of the bath, crying her eyes out. I held her and hugged her, but she seemed inconsolable. 'I'm just so shocked and hurt,' she said.

I felt a bit relieved that I'd told her but also a bit sorry, too, because it had clearly upset her so much.

I tried to comfort her. 'Well, it was a long time ago. It's over now.' She was struggling, though. She said later that she felt an overwhelming sense of betrayal by our father.

In June, Coleen gave birth to a daughter, Ciara, by Ray Fensome who's now become her second husband. Maureen, Amy, Julia and I did a summer season in Torquay with Joe Pasquale — such a very nice man — topping the bill, and then we came home to Blackpool. Brian still seemed a little as though he was on automatic pilot, just going through the paces, but I hoped it was a phase he'd pass through.

Then I was at a friend's party one night. Brian came straight from work and arrived after me, so I went and sat beside him to say hello — and he immediately muttered something and moved away. The same thing happened when I approached him again. I was getting fed up with all his moods. I wanted an explanation as to why he was behaving in this strange, remote way. I followed him into the kitchen.

I said, 'You're not being very friendly.'

He grunted. I wanted to provoke him into saying what was on his mind. So I said something I'll always regret: 'You don't love me any more, do you?'

He looked at me, such a cold, searching look. 'No,' he said, 'not the way I should.'

It was the beginning of the end.

14

When Love Goes Wrong...

When we got home, Brian went into the front room and started to make up a bed on the sofa. I stood in the doorway, desperately trying to make sense of it all.

'What do you mean you don't love me any more?' I asked.

He wouldn't meet my eye. 'I don't know if I've ever loved you,' he said.

I started shouting and screaming. 'So our whole life together has been a lie, has it? All the fabulous things you used to do and say . . . You never meant any of them?'

He was angry now. 'Oh, I meant them at the time.'

He had always loved me, and we both knew it, but that didn't mean everything was going to be fine. I knew, deep down, that something fundamental had changed and it made me sick with worry. This was the only man I'd ever loved and it was as if he'd built a brick wall around himself. It didn't matter whether I coaxed or cried: I couldn't reach him.

The girls were still at the party, so they

heard none of this. Nor did we refer to it again in the coming weeks. I felt as if my life had been put on hold as Brian and I got on with our work as though nothing had happened. However he began coming home later and later each evening. Some nights, I'd leave his dinner waiting on the kitchen table for him after I'd gone to bed. I'd hear him when he finally got back, sometimes in the middle of the night, so drunk he could barely stand up.

He'd always been quite a heavy drinker, but this was different. I didn't know where he'd been and he wouldn't tell me; and I didn't know if he'd been getting drunk on his own or with someone else. Either way, this wasn't innocent, social drinking with mates. This was the action of a man drinking to obliterate whatever was going on in his head. As it turned out, I was only half right. I could have confronted him again about his behaviour but, however foolish this may now sound, and although I took the situation seriously, I still believed it was only a phase, that he'd wake up one day and come to his senses.

By now, Brian had a part-time job looking after the books for Bloomfield, the local working men's club where we'd first met all those years ago. He'd often stay behind after work and have a few drinks with people he knew. Then a group of them would go on to a hotel called the Dutchman where all the show people went and where they'd be served with drinks until three or four in the morning. Part of this group included a woman and her husband, who I also knew but not as well as Brian did. I'd met them both socially and liked them. She was particularly easy to talk to, always very chatty, even a bit flirtatious, I'd say, if there was a man around. Her husband was similarly friendly but perhaps a bit more reserved than his wife. Then, out of the blue one day, Brian announced that he was off to Newcastle at the weekend and that he was giving a lift to this couple. I assumed he'd drop them off and then go and visit his dad. Two or three days later, Brian said that the husband couldn't make it, but the wife still wanted to go. I was fine about that; there was no reason not to be. Brian and I were still communicating. Although, things were a bit strained but I thought he was having no more than a mid-life wobble. I had no reason to believe that this long and happy marriage was seriously under threat.

So off he went. After a day, I hadn't heard from him, so I tried ringing him on his mobile. There was no reply but I left a message. Another day passed and still no word from Brian. Finally, I managed to track him down. I was feeling really anxious by this stage. Whenever one of us had been away from home in the past, we'd talked three or four times every day on the phone. I was beginning to wonder whether something had happened to him.

I said, 'Are you all right? I haven't been able to get through to you.'

'No,' he said, 'we've been on Holy Island. The reception's not great there.' He couldn't have sounded more matter-of-fact.

We? Holy Island? The place Brian and I had spent our magical honeymoon? A sliver of ice entered my heart. 'What do you mean 'we'?' I said. 'Who are you with?'

He told me he was with this woman. I didn't know what to say. 'We stayed at Shirley's house' — that's his sister's — 'and then we went across to Holy Island, for a couple of days.'

I said, 'What? You and her on your own?' This was beyond my comprehension. I went berserk. 'Well, you needn't think you're coming back here.'

Brian sounded genuinely surprised. 'Nothing happened between us,' he said. He's stuck to that story to this day — but he must have known what a betrayal that represented, whether or not they shared the same bed. Sex would be the least of it. Without my knowledge, he'd taken another woman to a place that could not have been more intimate, more special to him and me, to us.

I tried to remain icily calm when he finally got home, but I couldn't contain my feelings. The row erupted almost immediately. I didn't mince my words. 'I don't want you living under the same roof as me,' I shouted. 'I want you to pack your bags this instant and leave and never come back.'

Brian started to defend himself. 'Look,' he said. 'I needed a break. She just came along for the ride on the spur of the moment.' He must have seen the look on my face. 'Honestly. Nothing happened.'

I said, 'Brian, you've taken another woman to the very place that you chose for our honeymoon. You couldn't have done anything more hurtful if you'd tried. And you expect me to believe that all you did was show her the sights. Get out!' I was screaming now, I was so hurt. Then I realised we had to talk to Amy and Alex. 'We have to tell the girls,' I said.

So I called them down from their bedrooms. As soon as they appeared, I told them their father was moving out. 'Your father's leaving,' I said, 'because he says he doesn't love me any more.' I felt they were

299

owed the truth. They looked so crestfallen, I decided not to tell them that he had just spent the weekend on Holy Island with another woman — and, unsurprisingly, he didn't mention it, either. Alex started crying and Brian put out his arms to her. She crossed the room and sat on his knee as he cuddled her. I was crying, too, and Amy came to comfort me.

Then Brian put some of his things into an overnight bag, left the house and went to stay with the Bloomfield steward who had a house next door to the club.

Brian's behaviour was so unlike the husband I thought I knew, I had to find out more. I started asking around. It turned out that he and this other woman used to sit in a corner at the Dutchman or at the club and Brian would pour out his heart to her. Then he'd walk her home, holding her hand. They'd also been seen sitting in a park at three in the morning. I don't know where Kevin was when all this was going on. I think he worked shifts, so maybe he wasn't in the club or hotel most of the time.

A couple of days later, Brian came back to the house. He'd obviously been turning things over in his mind. 'Why should I have to move out?' he asked. 'This is as much my house as it is yours. If you don't like the situation, *you* can move out.'

I exploded. 'But I haven't done anything wrong,' I cried. 'You've just spent two days with another woman — in our honeymoon cottage, for all I know. I'm not going anywhere.'

'And nor am I,' he said.

It was stalemate for the next two or three days as I tried to ignore the man I'd been married to all these years. Finally, I couldn't take it any more. 'Look, Brian,' I said, 'you're acting as though you have nothing to apologise for. How on earth do you expect me tolerate this?'

He simply replied by saying, 'But I told you I didn't love you any more.' He seemed to think that, having said that, he was now a free agent. But he wasn't. He was still married to me — and, if I'm truthful, I thought he'd continue to be. Maybe he was having some sort of crisis that would pass. I made up my mind that, when the situation was a bit calmer, I'd suggest we go to marriage counselling and get to the root of the problem. More than twenty-five years couldn't be thrown away so lightly.

He had one more ace up his sleeve. 'You ought to tell the girls the *real* reason why I'm going,' he said.

'And what would that be?' I asked.

'Because of what your father did to you.' The sexual abuse I'd suffered had festered in Brian's mind, apparently, and he could never overcome the guilt he felt about the possible risk to which we had exposed first Amy and then Alex. It had all become more than he could bear and that's why, he said, he wanted to end the marriage. This sounded to me like something Brian was hiding behind, even though I accepted that it had cast a shadow over our lives, so I decided that I should talk to Amy and then Alex and tell them what had happened when I was a girl.

The next day I made up my mind to tell Amy, and her then boyfriend Mark, as well as Alex about what my father had done to me. I was a bag of nerves because I knew I was about to deliver a bombshell, a shocking piece of news that would shatter my girls' illusions about their beloved grandfather, but I felt it had to be done and planned to do it when we were calmly eating dinner.

'I haven't told you the full story,' I said, 'about why your father says he can't live with me any more.' Then I told them what had happened when I was twelve. They sat there open-mouthed. Both Amy and Alex obviously found it incredibly hard to reconcile what I was saying with their fond memories of the grandfather who, up until this minute, they'd uncomplicatedly adored.

'Your father,' I continued, 'says he can no longer live with the knowledge that your granddad sexually abused me when I was young. I told your dad all about it before we got married, but I always said that, if he ever told anyone, I'd deny it. For most of our marriage, Dad has lived with the guilt that we sometimes left you with your granddad, each of us knowing what he'd done when he and I were alone together all those years ago. Now it's come to a head and he wants to leave me for good.'

There seemed very little left to say. Brian was ending the marriage, I explained, because of the burden of guilt he felt about the consequences of my father's actions. I still didn't tell Amy and Alex at that stage about their father's trip to Holy Island; they'd had quite enough to digest as it was.

Amy particularly took the revelations about her grandfather very hard; she was extremely distressed. She'd loved and respected him. Now, in an instant, he'd been blackened in her eyes. She wasn't only angry with her grandfather; she was angry with me, too.

Initially Alex was very quiet. She was only fifteen so I think it took her a while for the full implications to sink in. But, gradually, I could see that she felt the same as her elder sister. Neither of them could understand, given the way I'd suffered, how I could have left either of them in my father's care. And they're right. It's indefensible.

'I could have been abused,' said Amy, 'and it would have been your fault.'

I replied that I had no excuses for what I did, and that I have to live with that for the rest of my life. I can't change the past. I can only apologise time and again for taking that risk, for putting both girls in the way of possible abuse. I never thought that Alex and Amy would cut me out of their lives as a result of it all, but I seriously worried that their anger could destroy their relationship with me. And it did for a bit. I think Amy felt that I might as well have left her in the middle of the motorway, a different kind of danger but just as reckless as the way I behaved. She crystallised my worst fears, and made me realise that my attitude had been that, although I'd acted irresponsibly, nothing bad had happened, that I'd got away with it. And that's not good enough.

Not long ago, I told her that I should have kept what happened to myself, then she'd still love her granddad the way she did before he died, but she insisted it was better that she knew the truth. Anyway, I realised, I had little choice because Brian was using it as a reason to turn his back on our marriage, so I'm certain he'd have told her the secret sooner or later. It was better, more appropriate, for the girls to hear it from me. He did discuss it with them later, apparently, and talked about his share of the guilt, but neither of them believes that it was the main reason for our marriage failing.

Now, Amy says she hates my father. If ever I say something about his good side, she scolds me. 'Mum,' she says, 'he was an incestuous paedophile.' She's very straightforward about that. It gets on her nerves, she tells me, if one of my sisters says anything complimentary or recalls a fond memory of our dad.

With hindsight, she does wonder whether she'd sometimes felt uncomfortable alone in his company, but she can't be sure whether that's an accurate memory or a general feeling of unease knowing what she now knows. She recalls one occasion when she was ill and he was babysitting her. She must have been eleven or twelve. She was lying on the couch in Waterloo Road and he was sitting in an armchair opposite her. He'd bought her lots of sweets and magazines and they were watching a film on television. Then he went to the toilet. When he walked back into the room, he came and sat on the couch and put her legs on his lap. He started rubbing her ankles. She was hot and restless and she didn't like him crowding her like that, so she kept trying to push him off with her feet. Eventually, he moved back to the armchair. Now, she wonders if something might have happened if she hadn't pushed him away. We'll never know.

Against the backdrop of all this distress and soul-searching, Brian found somewhere to live just a few doors down from the working men's club. On one occasion, I went round to the back of the house that contained the converted flat where Brian was living to deliver some of his mail. He wasn't there but I looked in the window. It was tiny and pretty depressing. It backed on to a supermarket car park. If I couldn't sleep at night, I'd drive to the empty car park at three in the morning and then get out and stand on a small brick wall to see if I could tell what Brian was up to. I was behaving like a madwoman.

He was in a very bad way at this point and I suspect he was having some sort of breakdown. Friends had reported that they'd seen him drinking alone in pubs always supping on a pint or a vodka and Coke. He'd see the girls but not regularly. They'd ask him if he was going to come back home or if we were going to divorce. He'd do little more than answer in riddles.

'I don't know,' he'd say. 'Who can foretell the future?'

He'd become unrecognisable from the man I'd married. If I'd met him for the first time at that point in his life, I wouldn't have had anything to do with him. We still spoke occasionally on the phone, usually in connection with the girls, but I couldn't be civil to him. I was so hurt by what he'd done. I just couldn't accept that he'd cast aside everything we'd had. I was angry, very, very angry, but I still wouldn't accept that our marriage couldn't somehow be salvaged. In my head — and in my heart — we'd had such a great marriage and I still loved him. Surely there was a way back.

One evening, I was out buying a pint of milk when I happened to see Brian climb into a taxi. My heart seemed to stop beating. Where was he going at this time of night — and by cab? I was in the car and I didn't hesitate. I followed him at a discreet distance. Eventually, he got out of the taxi at a Chinese takeaway, went in and bought some food and then walked a little way down the road and through an alleyway into one of two houses, I couldn't be sure which. There was a tricycle in the garden of one of them; the other was a bit dilapidated with a sheet instead of a

307

curtain at one window. It was midnight by now and I didn't want to knock on the wrong front door, so I decided to return home.

I phoned him the next day.

I said, 'I saw you last night, going into somebody's house with a Chinese takeaway.'

'Oh yes,' he said, 'that's where John Long lives. Were you following me?'

'Yes,' I said.

'So how do you feel now?' he asked.

'A bit like a lunatic,' I replied, truthfully. 'What do you expect?'

'Anyway,' he said, 'now you know.' And he put the phone down.

I've said it before, but never was it more true than at this moment. Work was to prove my saviour. If ever I needed to be taken out of myself, it was right now. Maureen and I were no longer performing as the Nolans, but we'd been booked to appear in a revival show called *Reelinandarockin'* with stars from the sixties like Gerry Marsden, Mike d'Abo, Dave Berry, Brian Poole, Dave Dee, and Mike Pender from The Searchers. We had no work and then we'd been approached by an agent we knew called Derek Franks who told us about this tour but who said he wouldn't insult us by offering it because the pay was poor. On the other hand, some money was better than none at all and the gig sounded fun. So we said yes. Maureen and I were only the backing singers, but we had a great time. On and off over the next couple of years, we toured the UK, three times in all; we took the show to Jersey; we did a stint on the *QE2*; we went to Australia twice and to New Zealand and Singapore, too. I loved being with my sister. She was such an incredible support to me as I tried to hold my emotions in check. We'd share the same room. We'd go out together during the day. We'd perform side by side each evening. But then all my sisters rallied round me in my hour of need. I remember I called Coleen out of the blue on one lonely evening and she immediately insisted I come round to her house where I talked and cried and talked some more.

Maureen and I were responsible for all the back-up singing and we loved it. We just sang harmonies and there was no pressure on us. They were probably no more than ten years older than us, but all these old rockers treated us like kids. They were so protective, so supportive. We also had a ten-minute spot on our own. It was fabulous and such a breath of fresh air after my cancer scare and the unravelling of my marriage. The show was also providing much-needed income. At this stage, Brian was still paying half the mortgage, but I had to pay all the other household bills and for the food I put on the table.

It was while we were away on one of these gigs that I got a call from Brian one day out of the blue. He was still living in his miserable little flat.

He said, 'I've just received a text from somebody saying, 'I bet your wife won't be in the mood for dancing now.' And I wanted to tell you.'

I told him I didn't know what he was talking about.

'Well, I've been taking this girl out,' he went on. 'Just a couple of times for a meal and to the races. Obviously, we've been seen together and now someone's sent this message making out you're not going to be happy.'

I couldn't be bothered with his nonsense. 'It's got nothing to do with me,' I said. 'Brian, we're not with each other any more. Why are you worrying? Just tell them to mind their own business.' But of course inside I felt desperately hurt and upset.

It didn't take me long to find out it had been this new girlfriend's house he'd been to with the Chinese takeaway. So I drove back to the road where I'd seen him and parked opposite the alleyway. In time, a woman who looked to be in her late thirties came out of one of the houses. She was small — no more than five foot — slim and dressed in jumper and jeans.

I got out of the car and ran across to her. My heart was hammering in my chest. I was curious to see at close hand the person who was, to all intents and purposes, my love rival.

I said, 'Hi, my name's Anne Wilson.'

She said, 'Oh, you're Brian's wife.' She didn't seem remotely threatened by me. She was cool, controlled. 'I feel so sorry for you. Come inside. We can have a chat.'

I looked at her. I remember thinking that she was obviously trying to be nice. Then I pulled myself together. 'I'm not being funny,' I said, 'but you're carrying on with my husband. I don't want to chat with you. I'm never going to be your friend. For what it's worth, though, you're welcome to my husband. Our marriage is over.'

The woman had no shame. 'Oh, I know that,' she said. 'He told me he's never loved you.' She had no idea whether Brian had said any such thing to me. 'Anyway,' she continued, 'he's filing for divorce.'

I pretended I was perfectly well aware of that, but it wasn't true. Brian had mentioned nothing about officially ending the marriage and, although I told her it was over, a part of me still hoped against hope that Brian and I

311

could salvage something from this nightmare situation. I stumbled back to the car, trying not to let her see my tears.

In a way, I got my own back — not that I planned it like that — when I confronted the two of them a few weeks later. They'd obviously been drinking, and I admit I was in a blind rage.

'Never mind about you filing for divorce,' I said, poking my finger at Brian. 'I'll get in before you — and I know who I'll be citing.'

'You do just that,' said his girlfriend. 'You can cite me. I'm not bothered.'

'Oh, I won't be citing you,' I said. 'I'll be citing the woman he took to Lindisfarne.'

That stopped her in her tracks. She looked at Brian and he just groaned.

I was later told by Ritchie, who'd always been a close mate of Brian's, that Brian had immediately taken his girlfriend round to the woman in question's house and had got her to swear that nothing had ever gone on between them.

That was no real victory, though. I'd been lashing out, trying to hurt the man I'd once loved so deeply. I wanted so much to reach him, to shake him out of what I fervently hoped would prove to be a temporary aberration.

I'd see his car parked outside the working

men's club and I'd go and ask if Brian was in the back office. I'd walk in and he'd be at his desk. He'd look horrendous: dishevelled, tired, unshaven, bleary-eyed. I remember I once marched in and sat down on the chair opposite him.

'What do you want?' he said. 'Go away!'

I said, 'No, I'm not going away, Brian. I want to talk to you.'

He started shouting, 'Leave me alone. Please go away. I can't handle this.'

But I wouldn't. I walked to the office door and closed it. 'Calm down,' I said. 'We need to talk. Do you love her?' I asked.

'Yes,' he said, 'I love her.'

'Are you in love with her, though?'

He hesitated for about ten seconds. 'Yes,' he said, eventually. 'Now leave here. Please.' And he put his head in his hands. I thought he was going to cry. 'I can't handle this,' he said. 'It's not fair.'

Up until then, I'd felt we could probably sort out our problems on our own, but now I could see him slipping away from me. I started crying uncontrollably.

'Could I have a hug, please?' I said, desperate for some kind of contact with him.

He came round from behind his desk and took me briefly in his arms. Then he pushed me towards the door. 'Right, now go!' he said.

Two nights after that incident, I woke up in the small hours, my head spinning. I came downstairs and started writing Brian a letter. I've still got a copy of it. I told him he was everything to me: my brother, my father, my lover, my husband, my best friend. He used to tell me that he couldn't wait until we grew old, so that we could sell the house and go round the world in our own Winnebago. 'What's happened to all of that?' I wrote. I also told him that when I sang 'Wind Beneath My Wings', I was singing it to him because the words so perfectly summed up our relationship. This was the first time that anything had ever gone wrong in our marriage. I implored him not to turn his back on it, on us. I know this was rather a Hollywood flourish but I begged him, 'Please don't let this be the way our story ends.' Finally, I told him that I felt he owed it to me and all the happy years we'd spent together to give marriage counselling at least one try. 'Whatever you want,' I said, 'we'll do it on your terms.' I was trying to be as flexible as I knew how.

Brian never acknowledged the letter, never replied to it. His silence was deafening. It seemed that he had no interest in trying to resurrect our marriage.

Emotionally, I was all over the place. I just

didn't know how I'd ever be able to think straight again, to get myself on an even keel. On one occasion soon afterwards, I phoned him ninety times in a single evening after I'd been out with friends and drunk too much. I'd get through to his answering machine, hang up and redial. Alone in the house, I'd hurl things at the wall. How dare he treat me like this! This was the man who was going to grow old with me.

I couldn't sleep. So I'd get in the car and go and park it outside his girlfriend's house and stare up at the bedroom window. She was ten years younger than Brian, sixteen years younger than me. One night, something inside me snapped. I was in the car and I was driving aimlessly around. It was raining hard, but I deliberately turned off the wipers and put my foot on the accelerator. I couldn't see anything beyond the windscreen. My life felt meaningless. I wanted out. I doubt I drove like that for more than thirty seconds, but I could have been killed and I could have killed someone else. It wasn't a rational act and I'm certainly not proud of it. Only thoughts of Amy and Alex left without their mother brought me back to something like my senses.

Even so, I couldn't get out of my head that Brian had been with me for twenty-seven years, married for twenty-four, a loving husband always there for me. He might have fallen out of love with me at the end, but ours had been such a happy marriage and he'd been a wonderful father. He couldn't do enough for his girls. So who knows what went wrong? I don't believe it was what my father had done and feel angry that this was Brian's reason for the breakdown. If he'd felt so bad about the prospect of Amy and Alex being left alone with their granddad, why did he stand by and let it happen?

I just can't accept that the guilt of his actions — or, rather, his lack of action as he stayed silent — preyed and preyed on his mind. Even if it had, why take it out on me? It wasn't my fault I'd been abused. I had nothing to defend myself with when he picked that up as a stick with which to beat me all those years later. It once again demonstrated how something as evil as what my father did to me never really goes away. I was abused at twelve. Here I was, over forty years later, and that abuse was indirectly responsible for ending my marriage to a man I loved with all of my heart.

Not that Brian seemed the same man any more. People would tell me that he looked a mess as he wandered the streets. He'd been officially diagnosed by this stage as clinically depressed: his doctor had prescribed a course of antidepressants. Brian would call members of my family and leave rambling messages. One day, he turned up at Maureen's house. 'You can do what you want,' he told her, 'but you Nolans are never going to get me.' The combination of trying to make a success of his business, our spiralling debts and the fact I'd been battling cancer had proved too much for him to handle.

Nor has he ever returned to being the man I knew and loved. The girls see him from time to time and they say he's changed. In a strange way, that's a comfort to me. I couldn't bear it if he'd gone back to being the old Brian and still didn't want to be with me. As it is, it seems to me he had a major midlife crisis which he survived, but it changed him for ever. I'll never get over it, though. I loved him so much. It seems unbelievable to me that it should come to this. How much happier do you have to be to stay together?

You can only divorce in less than five years by mutual consent, and, initially at least, I wasn't prepared to give him that consent. I didn't want the marriage to end and, while I wouldn't want him back now, I didn't see why I should make it easy for him. Any thought that I might do as he asked evaporated the moment I read his divorce petition. My eyes practically popped out of my head. It was horrendous. I didn't recognise most of what he was saying. When I showed it to my sisters and then to my daughters, they all reacted in the same way. They were horrified.

For legal reasons I can't say here what the petition claimed. Needless to say I deeply disagreed with the content and was terribly hurt by it.

It was too late now, though. I had to face it: my marriage was over.

Amy was at home one day when her father telephoned. He was worried, he said, that I'd go mad when I received the petition, so she better be prepared. She calmly replied that the petition had arrived a week earlier.

'What did she say?' Brian asked.

'Nothing,' said Amy. 'She just filed it away.'

The truth is that all the charges he'd laid at my door didn't make me angry; they made me sad. When I phoned him, I told him we both knew that none of what he'd claimed in the divorce petition was true.

'Oh, Brian,' I said. 'All I've ever loved is you and the kids. I'd never have done anything to further my career, as you put it, if it had meant jeopardising our marriage or upsetting our children.' He didn't reply, but what could he have said? He wouldn't budge, though, and I had little choice but to start getting on with the rest of my life.

I also had to live with the girls trying somehow to get to grips with what my father had done to me. When he was alive, they idolised him. Since his death and this dreadful revelation of his dark side, they've had to rewrite their history, and it's been hard for them. Amy was my parents' first grandchild. They both absolutely doted on her, and later on Alex, too. They loved all their grandchildren and those grandchildren loved them back. Now, their memories have been poisoned for ever.

But there are crumbs of comfort. Amy remembers all the times that her grandfather made disparaging remarks about her grand-mother. He'd say how Gran Nolan would nag him all the time, leaving the young Amy with the idea that my mum had been difficult. It's why she always felt that my father was the one she loved more. Now, she's been able to rewrite the past and rehabilitate her grand-mother.

I shared my mixed feelings with the girls about telling my story in print for the first time. Was it right, I wondered, to blacken their granddad's name? Neither of them was in any doubt. 'He deserves to have his name blackened,' said Amy. If love is blind, then so is pain, and I was terribly bruised by what had happened, but I wasn't alone. Amy and Alex were suffering too, and their anguish was a mix of anger and hurt and a feeling of betrayal. I think that at first they felt their dad and I hadn't loved them enough to protect them from my father, that we had exposed them to potential danger. And there we were all over again. A bad man does a bad thing to an innocent girl and, four decades and more later, two more innocent girls are caught in the crossfire, two more innocent victims are torn in half as they grapple with the implications of their own grandfather's wickedness. However, Amy says now that I was a victim and that there's no reason to feel guilty that my story will force people who knew and loved him to reassess the man. Not that everyone will be learning the true story for the first time. I quite quickly began to find out what Brian had been saying after he'd left me and was going through his breakdown.

Having told our daughters that he'd found it impossible to deal with the consequences of my father's abuse of me and his own mute acceptance of the same man babysitting them, Brian had nonetheless shared my story with friends. Perhaps he felt it would help with unburdening his guilt. Perhaps he couldn't help himself. Either way, it felt like it was a terrible betrayal of something that was intensely personal to the two of us. If anyone had the right to tell my story, it was me, not Brian.

It got worse. In time, I felt I wanted to tell my closest friends what had gone on all those years ago and yet, when I broached the subject with more than one of them — people who'd been close to both Brian and me — they revealed that he'd told them my story *years* ago. At the time, they hadn't known what to do, what to say, and hadn't felt able to tell me what he'd said. I don't blame them. But I do blame him.

Brian certainly hadn't shared with me the fact that he'd seen fit to tell people my story without first consulting me. He'd had no right to do that. This was my story, my experience, and I was the only person who should and could decide whether what had happened might be shared with anyone else. Another friend, a woman, was once told by Brian to watch out for her daughter if my father was around, but I never knew that at the time.

In his divorce petition, it was clear that Brian believed it was essentially my fault that the girls had been left with my dad. The implication was that I, more than anyone, knew how dangerous the consequences could be of so reckless a decision — and that poor

Brian had to struggle with his guilt as a result. He's right. I can never excuse the way I more or less trusted to luck in this regard. But, dear God, I think he should accept some responsibility, too.

15

Staying Alive

Quite soon after Brian moved out, my mother came to stay. It was only going to be for a few days initially but, in the end, she was there for six months. The girls and I could see her retreating into her own little world almost before our eyes. I remember waking up one night and Amy was in my room. She said, 'Listen, Mum. Gran's singing.'

It was four o'clock in the morning. I went to her room and she was sitting on the bed, looking down at the floor.

I said, 'Are you all right, Mum?'

'Oh yes,' she said. 'I've just been to the toilet.'

I knew she hadn't. Amy and I had been listening to her soaring soprano voice filling the house. It was weird and a little scary at that time of the night. So I spoke softly to her and calmed her down. She got back into bed and eventually fell asleep.

On another occasion, we took her out to a restaurant. For some reason, she got it into her head that they were trying to poison her, deliberately putting something in her food. She took one taste and hurled it across the restaurant. 'I know they're trying to kill me,' she said. Another time, she caught someone's eye, a perfectly innocent diner. 'What are you looking at?' she snarled and then started swearing, something she'd never done in her whole life. And this was heavy-duty swearing. If she'd been in her right mind, she'd have been horrified at herself. I must confess that it almost made me laugh because those words sounded so bizarre coming from her. We took her for any number of tests at the doctor's. The prognosis quite soon became clear: she was in the grip of Alzheimer's. With hindsight, we can all see that her condition started in Florida, although we misinter-preted it at the time. For instance, she'd go out each day with all her travellers' cheques unsigned in her handbag. We'd try and point out how risky that was, but she wouldn't listen. At the time, I thought she was just being stubborn.

The situation was becoming untenable. If I was sitting in the lounge at home with Mum and I went off to the toilet, I'd come back and she wouldn't be there. She'd have wandered into the hall, opened the front door and she'd be off down the street. Tommy, on his way to work, came across her at six o'clock one morning wandering though the centre of Blackpool in just her underskirt and a coat, nothing else. He brought her home to me, but we both knew that she needed twenty-four-hour care. She could not go back to the sheltered accommodation. Within the space of five minutes, she'd ask you the same question ten times, just like a small child. She and I were out on one occasion with Denise and her partner Tom, and we pulled into a car park so I could nip out and buy a bit of food in the supermarket. While I was away, Mum suddenly piped up, 'Oh Tom, this traffic's terrible. I don't think we've moved an inch in about an hour.' In the end, it was easier to agree with her. If you argued, she'd get all agitated.

We started taking her round any number of care homes in Blackpool, hoping that she'd like one of them. She hated them all, without exception. It was awful; we'd step over the threshold and she'd immediately start crying, 'I don't want to stay here. I don't like it here. I'm not old. I don't need to go into a home.' Then one day, for absolutely no logical reason, she walked into a home and announced that she really liked it. It was better than some, less good than others. Who knows why this one in particular should speak to her?

So she agreed to move in — but that wasn't the end of it. One of us would come to take her out for the day, but when it was time to return her to the home, something obviously stirred deep in her mind. 'Oh, why can't I come and stay with you?' she'd wail. At that stage, she clearly knew enough to realise that she didn't want to be there.

That phase had now passed. She did make friends with an elderly resident in the same home. His mind was alert but he was physically frail and couldn't have looked after himself on his own. Everything seemed to be fine with their relationship, and then I turned up one day and she was being verbally abusive to him, calling him all sorts of names. Poor man. I tried to explain that she didn't mean it, that she didn't know what she was saying.

She was deteriorating. If we took her anywhere to eat, I had to feed her. She had to drink through the sort of cup with a lid on it that a small child uses. She became incontinent and we'd have to take her to the toilet and clean her up as she screamed, 'I can't believe a daughter of mine is doing this to me.' The whole thing was wretched.

So we had moved her into a home, where she just lay in bed, unable to recognise her own children or watch television or do anything other than exist. We visited her two or three times a week without telling her we were coming, not because she'd have noticed one way or the other but because we wanted to see that she was being properly looked after and that the staff were just as kind to her when they didn't know we were about to turn up. And they were. Truly, these people were angels.

She remained there from the beginning of 2006 until her eventual death from bronchial pneumonia on December 30, 2007. She couldn't do anything for herself. The television was left on in her room which I was pleased about: maybe she could hear the music and that brought her some sort of comfort. But how could you tell? What I found hardest to bear was not knowing whether she was in pain. She couldn't communicate at all. I used to think it would have been wonderful if she could have gone to sleep one night and not wake up in the morning.

In the event, that's exactly what happened. I was sad when we got the news but I didn't cry. To be honest, it was a relief and a release. She'd always been very religious and believed — or she did when she was able to articulate it — that she'd be going to a better place when she left this world. I miss her terribly, of course, and will always remember how wonderful she'd been to me all my life. She was the sort of person who'd travel uncomplainingly from Blackpool or London to Paignton at a moment's notice to babysit for me when Amy was little. Any time I was in trouble or finding it hard to cope, she'd be on the next train. She always put us kids before herself.

Looking back now, part of me feels that perhaps it would have been better if my mother had known what my father had done to me because then it could have all been sorted out. Certainly, the whole business of leaving my girls with their grandfather would never have arisen. Perhaps it might even have had a positive effect on my marriage in that Brian couldn't have used it as an excuse to leave me. I'll never know. On the other hand, my mother had already been through a lot with my father and that revelation would have shattered her. I honestly don't see how she would have coped if she'd been told the truth. So part of me is pleased she was spared that.

⋆   ⋆   ⋆

Quite quickly, Brian stopped paying his half of the mortgage. He wasn't working; he couldn't. He was claiming disability benefit following his breakdown. I assume that went to the new woman in his life as a contribution to his living expenses. If ever I said I was strapped for cash, he'd say he was, too.

I opened a credit card account and struggled the best I could to meet the total mortgage repayment — over £500 a month — while also dealing with all the utility bills and the day-to-day running costs of three adults. Maureen and I were paid £306 between us per gig on the *Reelinandarockin'* tour, which helped on a daily basis, but the shows were sporadic: sometimes there'd be three or four a week, and then we'd go a month with no gigs at all.

There was one day, though, when both Alex and I earned a bit of pocket money and had a laugh into the bargain. The BBC was making a series called *Blackpool*, starring David Morrissey and Sarah Parish. It was a strange amalgam of musical, romance and thriller, a fantasy a bit in the style of Dennis Potter's *Pennies From Heaven*. I played a gypsy fortuneteller who pops out of her tent on North Pier in a dream sequence to tell David Morrissey's character what was going to happen to him, except that I did so in song. In fact, I was miming to somebody else's voice. Alex and her friends were extras, walking along the pier. She got £60 for the day and I got a little more.

It came in useful, but I was slowly sliding downwards, deeper into debt. So I did the only thing I could think of: I opened another credit card account to help pay off the first one, and so the problem snowballed. I kept all of this from my daughters and sisters at this stage. I'd just got to the upper limit of the second card when the tour promoters asked us to take a cut in wages. That always seems to happen: tour costs rise from one year to the next, but not ticket prices, and the artists are expected to subsidise the difference. It simply wasn't worth our while to go out on the road for what they were offering.

However, I got a summer season in Torquay in 2004 with Maureen, Amy and Julia. I'll always have happy memories of the town, and it was good to be earning regular money for eight weeks. I took Amy back to Torbay Hospital where she was born, and the same nurse who'd looked after me was still there twenty-three years later. Sadly, the surgeon, Mr McPherson, who'd almost certainly saved my life had since died, although there was a photograph of him in a frame hanging on the wall and I took a picture of Amy standing next to it.

After the summer season, and out of the

blue, I was offered a tour with Bobby Davro. Perhaps this would get me back in the black. The signs certainly looked good. The promoter didn't exactly inspire confidence, though. He was unkempt, he reeked of alcohol and he smelt. I was to be the principal female singer with four dancers, four backing singers and a seven-piece band. He would pay for all the equipment — the lights, the sound and so on — as well as all the transport and accommodation. I remember having a meeting with Bobby Davro and we were both worried. Tours on that scale just don't happen unless they're backed by big organisations with big money.

I was pretty nervous, not least because this was a solo outing for me — I wouldn't have Maureen standing next to me — but I was really excited about the prospect of working with Bobby on a major, twelve-week tour, and at the thought of making serious inroads into my debts. I was to be paid £500 for each show, but no expenses. This could be a real turning point. So I forked out a thousand pounds on clothes and jewellery and make-up, even Estee Lauder make-up brushes. I bought two long, beaded evening dresses from a shop on Bond Street in Blackpool and two pairs of smart shoes, one in silver, one in gold. I knew I had to look and give of my best.

After three gigs, however, we hadn't been paid a penny — and that's when the whole tour fell apart and the promoter went bankrupt. Maureen meanwhile had been cast in the role of Mrs Johnstone in the West End musical *Blood Brothers*. Naturally, I was delighted for her, but I had no bookings myself, and Amy and Alex were relying on me. Amy of course had been bringing some money into the household since she left school at sixteen via various jobs. For instance, she once worked as a guide at Sea Life, a local attraction, and then she was personal assistant to a company director. Alex was still at college although she did have a part-time job in a shoe shop that helped finance her own toiletries and so on.

Amy and I got jobs with a man who ran a company that helped people get compensation for personal injuries. The ethics were highly questionable. Its critics call this practice ambulance chasing and I was the ambulance chaser. I'd drive round the country, distributing leaflets and badges, keyrings and beer mats, advertising our services. I'd walk into A&E departments and leave them around, in the hope that people would then contact us and we'd get them a lump sum from which we'd deduct a percentage. It wasn't a particularly edifying way to make money, but I was desperate. I had two girls to support and a father who could not contribute. I got paid £200 a week for about six months. Then Amy and I both got a pantomime together in York, after which neither of us could face the idea of returning to our dodgy jobs, so I worked briefly for the local paper, promoting it in supermarkets, handing out free gifts. People would come up to me and say, 'Aren't you one of the Nolans?' And I'd say, 'Yeah, but I'm between jobs and a bit bored just sitting at home.' I kept a fixed smile pinned permanently to my face.

After that, I sold David Essex merchandise at the Opera House in Blackpool during his summer season. I'd met him years earlier because Linda and her Brian had been good friends of his manager. It was through her Brian that I got the merchandising job. I'd have jumped at the chance of anything. The money was good: £400 a week which certainly helped keep the wolf from the door, even if it didn't make serious inroads into my mountain of debt. Again, people would pass me when I was standing in the foyer of the theatre trying to sell my wares, do a double-take when they spotted my face and then come and ask if I once sang with the

Nolans. When I told them they were right, they'd ask how come I was doing this. I didn't tell them the truth, which was that I was prepared to do what I was doing for one simple reason: to put food on the table for me and my two children.

I've always regarded my time in show business as a gift. No one can take it away from me and I have all my memories. I've always been someone who lives in the present and, at the time — what with the cancer, the disintegration of my marriage, the winding down of my career and my spiralling debts — I was bumping along the bottom, so there wasn't much point being too proud to turn my hand to something else. I never felt that selling David Essex merchandise was beneath me. I saw it as a great opportunity to earn some much-needed cash.

In November 2005, I signed on for Job Seekers' allowance; that was just £52 a week. I went to a typists' agency, but I was never going to get a job for the very good reason that I couldn't type. I did a test once, but I was blagging it from start to finish, which they must have spotted a mile off. I made no secret of the fact that I'd been one of the Nolans, which interested some people, but it was clear that all I knew about was show business. I'd had no other experience.

I had to sign on once a fortnight. I'd apply for jobs as a dentist's receptionist or a doctor's receptionist, working in a shop — a bridal shop, a furniture shop, a department store, you name it — but they all of them, every last one, told me that they'd put me on their books and that, if anything came up, they'd be in touch. I heard nothing from any of them. No one wanted a woman in her mid-fifties who'd spent her life as a singer.

Then my luck changed. There was a girl called Karen Jones in the Job Seekers' branch in St Anne's who took a shine to me. She was wonderful, so motivational. 'I believe in you,' she said. 'You'll get something, I just know you will.' I was in there one day and she was scrolling down her computer screen. Suddenly, she skidded to a halt. 'Ah, now here's one for you,' she said. It was a job at the Insolvency Service at the Official Receiver's office — an irony that wasn't lost on me — that dealt with many of the cases of bankruptcy, both personal and commercial, which occur in the northwest. She told me I had the confidence to handle what they required, and much more organisational experience than I might imagine: when the act had been reduced to just Maureen and me, with Amy and Julia, I'd tended to be the one who'd booked the hotels, made the

335

travelling arrangements and sorted out the rehearsal schedule. Karen helped me fill in the application form and I was duly summoned for an interview. Two weeks later, I heard from them: I hadn't got the job, but they were putting my name on their reserve list. Well, I knew what that meant. They were being polite and I'd never hear from them again.

A week later I got a call from a friend. She'd had a letter from the Insolvency Service asking her for a reference. The next day, I got an identical call from another friend who I'd nominated as a referee. Two days later, the Service wrote to me and said the job was mine if I wanted it. I couldn't believe it. I began working for them in June 2006. Initially, I was responsible for sorting the post and distributing it, which I liked because it meant I was on my feet the whole time and never sitting at a desk, watching the clock. I also had to store and retrieve files. Then I was promoted at the end of last summer, and now I'm dealing with the bankrupts direct on the phone.

I'm happy there. Everyone knows what I used to do and sometimes they'll ask about my former life. I don't mind discussing it, but it feels as if I'm talking about someone from another planet. What I like best about the job is the guarantee of regular money at the end of each month, which means I can budget for all my household expenses. I got used to the unpredictability of show business, but, at this stage of my life, a little security is no bad thing.

Around the same time as I got my job, I had to sell the house on Falmouth Road as I was no longer able to make the monthly mortgage repayments. A man who lived opposite said he'd buy it for cash, although at less than the asking price. Then someone who'd played football with Brian when he'd been part of the Blackpool team offered to pay me £10,000 more than my neighbour. I was desperate to make a quick sale, because I'd now had a letter from the mortgage company telling me the house was about to be repossessed. There was also the further complication of Brian having to sign the papers, because we owned the house jointly.

Negotiations were dragging, with each set of solicitors blaming the other side as the day for repossession drew nearer and nearer. I rang the building society to ask for a little more time, but they refused. So my solicitor rang the courts and asked for a meeting with a judge who might grant me a stay of execution. An appointment was made for the next morning, the very day when the house was due to be repossessed at 12.30. We got there at nine o'clock, but didn't get to see the judge until 11.30. It was totally nerve-racking; time was literally running out. Unless I could stop the repossession and sell the house for £110,000, I'd have to be declared bankrupt.

The judge gave us an extension of two hours, just long enough in the event for all the relevant papers to be signed. To this day, I can't adequately describe the sense of relief that flooded through me when we squeezed in under the wire.

I found packing up to leave the house very traumatic. This had once been such a happy home. When I made the final journey to pick up my remaining bits and pieces, I looked into the front room for the last time. There was a pile of stuff I didn't have the space for that was destined for the council tip. It all seemed so sad. I sank to the floor and sobbed my heart out. Had it really come to this? I tried to tell myself it could have been worse. I was so lucky to be moving to my Aunt Teresa's. The woman's a saint. She paid to have an extension built on to the back of her house so that Amy, Alex and I would be sure to have a roof over our heads. If one of the kids wants to borrow a tenner, she never refuses. Her kindness is beyond words.

After all the debts were paid, Brian and I were left with £38,000 to divide up between us. It wasn't a 50/50 split as I'd been the only one repaying the mortgage after he moved out from the house and from the marriage that I never wanted to end.

Eventually, after much wrangling, we came to an agreement. Better in the end to reach what the Americans call closure. At least, that way I've been able to move forward again. I've settled all my credit card bills. I've got a job that keeps me busy and pays me a regular wage. It's a million miles away from the life I once knew, but I'm only too well aware that there are so many people worse off than me.

In the autumn of 2006, after I started working at the Insolvency Service, I got an eight-week residency to sing two forty-minute solo sets once a week at the Blackpool Hilton. I did everything from Barbra Streisand songs to our own hits. I had the backing track of my sisters singing 'I'm In The Mood For Dancing', so I included that because people expect it of you. I was paid £200 per performance. Singing a long solo set after all those years surrounded by my sisters felt a bit strange and it's not something I'd particularly repeat in a hurry, but I love singing and I liked the extra money.

I've also done some charity appearances

since, and we all sang at my brother Brian's wedding to Annie last year; singing five-part harmonies again was a real treat. Then we were on *Loose Women* at the end of last summer. Coleen's a regular on the programme, so the producers had the idea of our closing the season by doing a song together. Apparently everyone at the Insolvency Centre piled into the kitchen at work and watched me on the TV. We had lots of letters after that appearance asking us to re-form, which was lovely, but we never will. We've all gone off in different directions and I can't honestly see us being able to make joint decisions and sticking to them now. In short, I think we'd probably end up killing each other! We see each other all the time, though; we all live within a mile radius of one another.

Denise does a lot of cruise work now, and corporate gigs. Maureen has been touring in a show called *Girls Behind* about three girls working the clubs. Sadly, Linda lost her husband Brian last September to liver and kidney failure which hit her very hard indeed, especially because she has been bravely battling breast cancer. Bernie's done a tour of a play called *Mum's the Word*, and she gets lots of acting jobs on television; she did a long spell on *Brookside* and then on *The Bill*.

Coleen's currently the most successful of the lot with her regular appearances on *Loose Women*, her TV adverts and her newspaper and magazine columns. Tommy makes his living these days by playing drums, and for some years he's also acted as a mentor to a young lad with special needs and guided him all the way from junior school through to college. Brian works as a sales rep.

It's now eight years since I was diagnosed with cancer, and there's been no recurrence of any health problems. I passed the crucial five-year mark in 2005 and, while you can never become complacent, I'm hoping the worst is behind me. My abiding sadness is the collapse of my marriage. It's the worst thing that has ever happened to me and that includes the abuse my father subjected me to. To rub a bit of extra salt in the wound, my divorce was finalised on 23 June 2007, the day that Brian and I would have been celebrating our twenty-eighth wedding anniversary.

I'm still angry with Brian for not giving the marriage one more go. We never see each other now — except by chance in the street — and he never gets in touch. I'll ask the girls how he's doing, but his attitude seems to be that somehow I never existed. That's hard to bear. I don't text him or phone him. I leave him to get on with his own life as I'm getting on with mine.

On good days, I recognise that the anger is slowly subsiding. Life's too short. I've been out with a couple of men since Brian and I broke up, just for a drink or a meal. The trouble is that I regarded Brian as my mate for life. I married him in a Catholic church and I meant what I said when I made my vows. It's hard to imagine I could meet someone else and fall in love, but you never know: after all, I couldn't have predicted that I'd get cancer or that my marriage would fail. We think we're in charge of our own destiny, but that clearly isn't the case. So, if someone said to me that the other great love of my life is out there and, when we meet, we'll live happily ever after, I couldn't dismiss it entirely. It doesn't seem very likely, but it's not impossible. In a few more years, it would be nice if there was a special man in my life, and it would be lovely if there was a grandchild or two. I hope, too, that by then Brian and I would have found a way to be friends again. I don't want to carry round this bitterness for the rest of my days.

Do I have regrets? Of course. I've had an incredible life which I've lived to the full, but my two major regrets concern the two men I loved unconditionally, both of whom let me down. It wasn't my fault that my father abused me and forever sacrificed my love for him. I was the victim and victims can't have regrets; they're the passive partner in a relationship. I'm sad that I couldn't have a normal father/daughter relationship. I do regret that I didn't confront what he'd done to me when my daughters were born. If I could turn back the clock, I wouldn't let the situation drift the way I did. I certainly regret whatever it was I did that meant my marriage didn't ultimately survive.

I have my beautiful girls, though, and they mean all the world to me. I have my memories of a wonderful career which took me from Dublin all round the world. I now have a job that has turned my life around. I also have what I hope will be a contented life to look forward to. Truly, I'm not complaining. Contentment, in my opinion, is vastly underrated.

We do hope that you have enjoyed reading this large print book.

Did you know that all of our titles are available for purchase?

We publish a wide range of high quality large print books including:
Romances, Mysteries, Classics
General Fiction
Non Fiction and Westerns

Special interest titles available in large print are:
The Little Oxford Dictionary
Music Book
Song Book
Hymn Book
Service Book

Also available from us courtesy of Oxford University Press:
Young Readers' Dictionary
(large print edition)
Young Readers' Thesaurus
(large print edition)

For further information or a free brochure, please contact us at:
Ulverscroft Large Print Books Ltd.,
The Green, Bradgate Road, Anstey,
Leicester, LE7 7FU, England.
Tel: (00 44) 0116 236 4325
Fax: (00 44) 0116 234 0205

Other titles published by
The House of Ulverscroft:

MY FATHER'S ROSES

N. Kohner

Nancy's grandparents and their three children find their sanctuary in the garden of the small town where they live — between Prague and the German border. There they have their happiest times — when the eldest son returns from the trenches of World War I, when their youngest son joins them in the family furniture business, and when their daughter gives birth to their first grandchild. But when the Nazi Storm Troopers march into Podersam their lives will never be the same again . . .

THE BOY WHO LOVED BOOKS

John Sutherland

John Sutherland's childhood ended before it began: when his father was killed flying a Wellington bomber. Half-orphaned, John was abandoned when his widowed mother decamped to Argentina with a new man. He was brought up by an assortment of well-meaning relatives and had an odd, unsettled childhood. He took refuge in books. But then his solitary reading habit merged into a bad drinking habit. *The Boy Who Loved Books* is the story of one man's, often desperate, love affair with reading matter; with drink and with an adored, but absent, parent. And during the shifting twentieth century, when profound changes shook society, it is also a personal account of what it was like to be a grammar-school boy, a national-service man and a redbrick graduate.

THE ACCIDENTAL ANGLER

Charles Rangeley-Wilson

Fishing can take you to the heart of a landscape — whether in the world's most outlandish and awe-inspiring places, or just at the end of your road, it will introduce you to the locals, rip-tides, floods, droughts — and, of course, fantastic slippery beasts. In *The Accidental Angler* you'll battle titanic monsters on a tropical atoll; chase inscrutable grayling through back gardens in Provence; dance in Brazilian carnivals, and find secret rivers hidden beneath the streets. Join Charles Rangeley-Wilson — angler, conservationist, television presenter and traveller — on a journey that will make the familiar new, and the strange familiar.

A VERY BRITISH COOP

Mark Collings

Mark Collings had rated pigeons the lowest of the bird family until he met Les Green, head of the UK top pigeon-racing team — known as the 'Salford Mafia' . . . Les, a sharp-tongued ex-gang member, is the author's guide through the weird and wonderful world of British pigeon racing. Pigeons are big business: there are 60,000 pigeon racers in the UK, and rivalry can provoke arson attacks on lofts. *A Very British Coop* is the story of a journey taken from a pigeon loft in Oldham to a shot at the ultimate prize — The Sun City Million Dollar Classic.

CHARLOTTE AND LEOPOLD

James Chambers

Charlotte & Leopold tells the story of the doomed romance between Charlotte, heir to the English throne, and Leopold, uncle to Queen Victoria and first King of the Belgians. Charlotte was the only legitimate royal child of her generation, and her death in childbirth was followed by an unseemly scramble to produce a substitute heir. Queen Victoria was the product. Charlotte won the hearts of her subjects. Yet, she was used, abused and victimised by rivalries — between her parents; between her father (the Prince Regent, later George IV) and (Mad King) George III; between her tutors, governesses and other members of her discordant household; and ultimately between the Whig opposition and the Tory government . . .

FIGHT THE GOOD FIGHT

Catherine Fox

Catherine Fox is not your typical martial artist. Her initiation into the sacred rites of judo began not in a dojo but in the Tunnel Cement Works in Pitstone, Buckinghamshire. And her dedication to the sport has been questionable: a thirty-year sabbatical, two children and a life spent writing books does not prepare one for enlightenment, or for beating your opponent on a padded mat. However, Catherine has set herself a challenge: before she turns forty-five she will become a black belt. After all, how many other vicars' wives get to roll around on the floor with sweaty blokes?